THE FORTIFIED HOUSE
IN SCOTLAND

THE FORTIFIED HOUSE
IN SCOTLAND

NIGEL TRANTER

VOLUME TWO

CENTRAL SCOTLAND

JAMES THIN

1986

THE MERCAT PRESS, EDINBURGH

ISBN No. 0901824 43 7

Printed by Billing & Sons Limited
Worcester

PREFACE

THE area covered by this second volume of *The Fortified House in Scotland* consists of the counties of Stirling, Clackmannan, Kinross, Fife and Perth, a belt of country stretching from the Clyde estuary to the North Sea. Being in the main a richly fertile area and with no great modern cities within it to overwhelm the countryside—although South Stirlingshire and West Fife are highly industrialised—it has remained rich in the class of building here dealt with. Perthshire, in especial, has proved notably productive.

The author has made every effort to ensure that the list of buildings included is as complete as possible. In the case of Perthshire especially, this has proved a major task, there being in existence no even semi-authoritative register, inventory or catalogue of such edifices, nor any comprehensive topographical and historical works dealing incidentally with this subject. Even parish histories, frequently a rich source of clues, are scanty and very inadequate. As well as much research, therefore, the finding of these houses has entailed a great deal of travel and local enquiry into every parish of the area. Buildings erected as townhouses, such as The Palace, at Culross, have not been included—as distinct from those houses round which towns have extended.

The tower-house, the defensive residence, the small castellated mansion, with which this book deals, is a category of historical monuments in which Scotland is uniquely rich, owing to a variety of coincidental historical causes. Centralised control on the part of authority came late to Scotland, as did the Reformation; the vast church lands were being apportioned out to a new class of smaller landowners at a time when fortified houses were nowhere else being required or erected in Europe. Here they were not only necessary but mandatory, the Crown insisting that such be built as one condition of granting the charters for the land, with a view to assisting in the pacification of the country; whether in fact they achieved this laudable end and did not rather add to the truculence of their independent-minded lairds, is today neither here nor there. But all over Scotland, in the late 16th and early 17th centuries especially, these sturdy and attractive defensive stone houses went up in their hundreds, almost their thousands.

[5]

Their numbers were quite extraordinary, especially considering the much smaller population of those days—proof if that was needed that in Scotland a notably large proportion of the people considered themselves to be of the gentry and lesser nobility. In Dumfriesshire alone, for instance, in 1590 there were over 130 of these fortalices, and in Peeblesshire over 80. The attractiveness of these houses was greatly enhanced by another historical coincidence, namely the French influence of the Auld Alliance reinforced by the Regency of Queen Mary of Guise and the reign of her French-educated daughter Mary Queen of Scots, plus the long minority of James Sixth, all of whom brought in so much help from France to aid them in the government of this country. Much that was lightsome and delicate in the notable château architecture of France thus became wedded to the more sternly functional and enduring Scots traditional style, to form one of the most happy and successful marriages in the architectural world —this development coinciding with the aforementioned Reformation redistribution of lands. There is just no comparison between the flowering of Scottish fortalice building of this period, and those towers erected in the North of England as defence against the Scots, these latter marked by a square and squat sameness and complete lack of flourish.

In these little castles, the new laird class of 400 years ago in Scotland grew up, liberally adorning their houses with carved heraldic panels and painted ceilings, as well as the corbelling, pepper-box turrets, crowstepped gabling, stringcourses and other typical features of the tower-house which are such a delight and treasure to us today. For these houses were built to endure.

Unfortunately, the other side of the picture is less happy. Although there were, and are, so many of these buildings, the wastage in them today is grievous and deplorable, indeed disgraceful. They are very much a wasting, though irreplaceable, asset. Although we are the envy of so many from lands less favoured in this respect, all too few of our own people either know, appreciate, or care for them. Especially, unhappily, local authorities, into whose hands many of them fall. Present-day conditions, although requiring the maintenance of tradition as never before, are against such buildings. The hands of the improver, the moderniser, the demolisher and the vandal are set against them.

There are fortalices illustrated here which will almost certainly not be in existence when this reaches print. Yet the country was never so rich. Is 20th-century Scotland to fail its forefathers and its posterity both?

CONTENTS

[9]

CLACKMANNANSHIRE

ALLOA TOWER

This massive and lofty tower of probably the 15th century stands in the grounds of the more modern Alloa House, close to the town. It has many unusual features, but unfortunately has been greatly altered, externally and internally. The vast number of symmetrically-placed windows which have been opened out—at enormous labour, since the walls reach a thickness of eleven feet —no doubt greatly add to the light of the interior, but much detract from the authentic aspect of the castle. It may be noted, however, that whichever Earl of Mar was responsible for this 'improvement' must have been of an unusually precise turn of mind, for the end windows of each row are in fact only dummies.

The building rises to four main storeys and a garret within the parapet. This parapet is unusual in that it rises flush with the walling, and is not projected on corbelling; also the crenallations are more elaborate than normal. There are open rounds at each angle, with a fifth in the centre of the northern wallhead, presumably for the additional protection of the door directly beneath. These rounds are provided with shot-holes. The parapet-walk is wide, owing to the extremely thick walling of good coursed rubble. A turnpike stair rises in the thickness of the south-west angle, and terminates in a conical-roofed caphouse at parapet-level. At the eastern end of the walk is a garderobe for the use of the watch.

Internally the building has been greatly altered, only the third floor being more or less as originally. This is a large chamber, 43 by 22 feet, the original windows in the centre of each wall having window-seats—but these have been widened in the 17th century when all the other windows were added. There are two fireplaces, but these are also of the 17th century. In one window

embrasure is a wall-closet with stone seat, flue, its own little
window and a lamp-recess.

The entrance, now covered by a Renaissance doorway, is in
the centre of the north front. The ground floor is vaulted. The
first floor chamber would be the Hall, and this has mural passages
in each of the lateral walls, that to the south leading to the turnpike stair in the south-west angle, which serves all floors above
the first.

Certain accounts say that the tower was built about 1223, but
while there may well have been a castle on the site then, the
present building as a whole is obviously considerably later. The
property was conferred on Sir Robert Erskine, Great Chamberlain of Scotland, by David Second in 1360, and has remained
with that great family, Earls of Mar, ever since, the seventh
after the Chamberlain being created Earl of Mar in 1565. The
family were ever the trusted friends of the Stewart kings, and
being Hereditary Keepers of Stirling Castle nearby, were apt to
be the custodians of the young princes in troubled days. James
Sixth, in especial, spent much time here as a child, Johnny Mar
being his closest companion.

CASTLE CAMPBELL

This well-known and impressive fortalice is commandingly situated about one mile north of the town of Dollar, high on a rocky spur of the Ochil Hills. Its position is one of great natural strength enhanced by artifice, crowning a mound between two deep wooded ravines, the burns of which are known as Sorrow and Care. The original name of the castle itself was The Gloume, or the Castle of Gloom. Why all this emphasis on sadness and misery it is hard to say, for the site and scene is a very lovely one—although strangely enough our forefathers did tend to equate the grandeur of mountain and rock scenery with sorrow and foreboding. Dollar itself was originally Doleur.

The building itself, partly ruinous, is a composite one, grouped in courtyard form round the original tall free-standing tower of probably the 14th century. There is no space here to describe all the various additions and extensions; it must suffice to say that there were considerable alterations and additions in the 16th and 17th centuries, and that the earlier tower itself was much altered on these occasions.

The entrance to the enclosure is by an arched pend to the north, above which there would originally be a gatehouse. The tower or keep is oblong on plan, and rises through four storeys to the parapet. The roof is flat, and may well always have been so, for the upper storey is vaulted—although this vaulting is not original. Where the top storey was vaulted, it was quite normal to have a stone platform roof resting thereon, within the parapet. There are open rounds at the parapet angles.

The keep has now two doors, the original being that in the west wall, at basement level, which gives access to the vaulted ground floor chamber, and also to a little straight stair in the thickness of the wall leading up to the first floor. The other door is at first floor level, and has been reached by an outside forestair, no doubt removable for defence. This is now reached, however, by the later stair-tower which dates from the late 16th or early 17th century. This stair-tower, built against the south-east corner of the keep, rises to parapet level, where it finishes in an ugly modern fashion. The original main stair was in the opposite south-west angle, in the thickness of the wall, and would no doubt end in the

usual caphouse-cum-watchtower, now no more. This stairway
has been long disused.

The Hall on the first floor is also vaulted, and is provided with
an arched fireplace, a buffet with an ogival head, and in the thickness of the east wall a pit or prison, a hatch in the stone flooring
leading down to this unpleasant hole at ground level. The second
floor is not vaulted, but as has been mentioned, the third or top
floor is, with elaborate barrel vaulting of late date. The entire
building is well provided with garderobes and mural chambers
in the very thick walls, typical of the period.

Much of the secondary work in the additions has been of a
very high standard, understandable considering the lofty rank of
its builders, including much fine stonework, mullioning and a
notable loggia.

The name was altered to Castle Campbell when the property
came into the possession of the Earl of Argyll, Chancellor of
Scotland, at the end of the 15th century. In those days the Court
centred round Stirling and Falkland, and no doubt successive
Earls of Argyll found this castle much more convenient as a base
than their traditional stronghold in the West. Here John Knox
stayed and dispensed the Lord's Supper on a great occasion in
1556, in the presence of the 4th Earl. The castle was burned by
Montrose's allies, as was Menstrie nearby, in 1645.

CLACKMANNAN TOWER

Set squarely on the top of a hill above the ancient town of Clackmannan, and a prominent landmark for miles around amongst the levels of the Forth, stands the tall and impressive tower of the Bruces. Traditionally said to have been built by King Robert himself, this is probably not so—although the oldest portion does date from the 14th century. This is the lower half of the north tower. Above that level the stonework is slightly intaken (as may be seen in sketch) and this is 15th-century work. The castle and barony of Clackmannan were granted to a later Robert Bruce by his cousin, King David, in 1359, and probably he it was who built the oldest work now found here.

The tower has grown and been altered through the centuries. To the south of the oldest part, a still taller tower, rising to 79 feet, has been attached in the late 15th century. This is built in a warm-coloured dressed stone, while the older block is constructed of grey coursed rubble. The addition is not so broad as the original, making an L-planned whole. There are indications of a courtyard, ditch, dry presumably from its hill-top position, and drawbridge.

The original entrance to the old tower was at first floor level, no doubt by a removable timber stair, but when the later tower was added a turnpike stair was built in the angle between, partly in old and new work. The doorway was placed at its foot. Later doors were opened in the east and west fronts, the former having an elaborate 17th-century surround, and machicolated projections built out high above them for their defence.

The main tower rises to four storeys and an attic, with the wing rising a storey higher. The tower is in a fair state of preservation.

To describe the interior would take much more space than is available. The ground floors are both vaulted, and had entresols or half-floors within the vaults. Both first floors are also vaulted, that in the main block being the Hall, with a fine 16th-century fireplace. There are many closets and garderobes contrived within the thickness of the walling, and at third floor level is an especially interesting feature—a remarkable long gallery within the walling, entered from one of the window embrasures.

The turnpike stair ends, at parapet-level, in a plain caphouse.

There is another little spiral stair in the re-entrant giving access from the lower parapet to the higher, also ending in a caphouse, this time surmounted by a belfry. There is also a brazier for a warning fire—and it is noteworthy that many other Bruce castles and strengths in the vicinity, such as Kennet, Garlet, Stenhouse, Airth, Auchenbowie, Carnock, Kinnaird, and so on, would be able to see such a beacon-light. The two parapets are carried on corbelling, that in the later wing machicolated for the casting down of missiles on to unwelcome guests.

Whether or not King Robert built any of the work here, Clackmannan was a royal hunting ground, and the family held the hereditory positions of Sheriffs and Foresters of the Sheriffdom of Clackmannan. It is interesting to note that here, the widow of the last laird, an ardent Jacobite, knighted Robert Burns with the two-handed sword of the great Robert the Bruce.

MENSTRIE CASTLE

This highly unusual and interesting old mansion, dating from the late 16th and early 17th centuries, was recently the subject of one of the many struggles that have to be waged to prevent our local authorities from demolishing and casting down our heritage of stone in the name of progress, after generations of neglect. Having fallen on evil days, and become a very sub-standard tenement, Menstrie Castle was doomed, had not people of goodwill rallied to its aid, and from as far away as Canada, with which country this house has an especial link. Despite the reluctance of the authority, the castle is now not only restored, occupied and a centre-piece of the housing scheme for the space of which it was to be demolished, but is indeed the showpiece and pride thereof—a wonderful example to other municipalities of what may be done with traditional buildings.

The house appears originally to have been quite a small L-shaped fortalice, but later the wing was extended, another wing was added, and a curtain wall erected to the east to join up, thus enclosing quite a large courtyard. The entrance to this was not in the curtain wall, as is usual, but by means of an arched passage or pend driven through the west front. The building is two storeys and an attic in height, with the gables crowstepped. An angle-turret, with gunloops, crowns the south-east corner, and there is a rather unusual corbelled-out stair-turret on the west front, its stair giving access between first and second floors only. More modern outside stairs rise to the first floor. Within the courtyard, in the re-entrant angle between the west and south wings, was a circular stair-tower, now removed. Moulded string-courses ornament both sides of the long west wing.

The entrance to the archway is by a handsome decorative doorway. Within the passage are stone benches, and on either side are vaulted chambers. Inevitably there has been great internal alteration during the house's vicissitudes. The curtain walling and all other secondary outbuildings have now been swept away, leaving only the bare west and south wings of the original house.

Menstrie was the country home of a very famous family, the Alexanders, one of whom became first Earl of Stirling and founder of Nova Scotia. He was born in this house in 1572. The origin of the Alexander family is particularly interesting, being a reversal of the usual process. They were chiefs of Clan Allister, and came from Kintyre with the Earl of Argyll who took up residence at Castle Campbell not far away, settling down at Menstrie about 1481. In a few generations they had become prosperous and powerful in Stirling and vicinity. A son of William, first Earl of Stirling, was Sir Anthony Alexander who became Master of Works for Scotland and Royal Surveyor, and eventually Warden of the Master Tradesmen of Scotland, receiving therefrom half the apprenticeship fees and fines. Menstrie was burned by Montrose in 1645 in consequence of the Alexanders' support of Argyll—at the same time as was Castle Campbell itself. Here was born, in a later century, Sir Ralph Abercromby, the hero of Aboukir.

The castle stands, surrounded now by modern housing, within the village of Menstrie directly under the escarpment of the Ochil Hills, five miles north-east of Stirling.

SAUCHIE TOWER

This sturdy and well-planned fortalice is not to be confused with that of Little Sauchie, or Sauchieburn, in Stirlingshire. It stands on rising ground a short way north of the mining village of New Sauchie, two miles north-east of Alloa, and is an almost square tower of 15th century construction within a ruined courtyard in which 17th century and later buildings have been erected.

The keep is substantial and exceptionally well-constructed of good ashlar, and contains beneath the parapet four main floors and an entresol or half-storey. There has been a further garret storey within the gabled roof above, but this has now collapsed.

The entrance is at ground level in the west front, through an arched doorway, leading into a mural lobby. To the left, in the north-west angle, rises the turnpike stair, which eventually terminates at parapet level in a hexagonal and conical-roofed caphouse. To the right a small guardroom has been contrived in the thickness of the walling. The ground floor has a high vaulted ceiling, with corbels still projecting at the springing of the vault, to carry the beams for an entresol or half-floor. This entresol has been better lighted than the main basement below, the window in the south wall having been provided with stone seats; below there are only slits in the masonry. These entresols were frequently used in early times for the sleeping accommodation of men-at-arms and servants, who presumably were not in a position to object to low-roofed cramped quarters. The basement below could be used either for storage or for cattle.

A tiny vaulted mural chamber, reached from the basement, has been excavated in the very thick west wall—possibly as a pit or prison. Above this, still in the west wall, is another longer but narrow mural chamber, provided with two windows. This strange place seems to have become the bakehouse, however ill-designed for the purpose, and the garderobe or closet at the south end converted into an oven. On the first main floor, as usual, was the Hall. This has been a fine apartment, provided with a great fireplace 8½ feet wide, stone seats in the three windows, with lockers, and a wall-closet with a stone basin in the north wall. The large window to the west still retains its great iron yett, and off the embrasure of this window is still another mural chamber, with a service-hatch to the Hall itself.

The second and third floors, now unfortunately fallen in, have been slightly larger than those below, owing to the thick walling being somewhat backset to provide more space. These two storeys are both equally well provided with wall-closets and window-seats, the walling of the entire tower being honeycombed with mural chambers. Its designer seems to have been of an ingenious turn of mind, with something of an eye for labour-saving devices.

The parapet is carried on individual corbels, and there are open rounds at all four angles. Although the gables have now largely fallen in, part of that at the north end remains, and reveals a most unusual device; the gable-end has been built very wide, and its crowsteps used to form a stairway to a snug position behind the caphouse roof, utilised as a look-out post.

It is unfortunate that this most interesting castle is not in a better state of preservation. Sauchie was long the seat of the family of Shaw, or Schaw, whose name is perpetuated in Schaw-park nearby. By marriage they, in 1420 acquired the property from a family named Annand. James Schaw of 'Salquhy' had a letter from the King in 1480, in the Exchequer Rolls. He was Tutor to the young James the Fourth. Charles Schaw, Lord Cathcart, was served heir of his grandfather, Sir John Schaw, in 1753. The Schaws were masters of the King's Wine-cellar, and their arms show three covered cups.

FIFE

ABERDOUR CASTLE

Only the extreme eastern range of this once great and important castle remains fairly entire. Space forbids any comprehensive description of the other extensive ruins that centre round the massive 14th century keep; this was all accidentally burned in the 18th century, and thereafter used as a quarry.

This easternmost portion dates from the early 17th century, with somewhat later alterations. It consists of a long oblong main block, with two small projections to the north and a square wing jutting southwards—the part drawn in sketch. In the re-entrant between south wing and main block rises a low squared tower, containing the entrance and a stairway. The roofing of this range has been lowered, with somewhat unsightly effect. The masonry is in general coursed rubble, but ashlar in the south wing, with the windows enhanced by good mouldings. It is possible that this wing represents the remains of a former flanking tower of a large courtyard, on to which the later main block was grafted. This is only two storeys high, the wing rising a further storey. What have been dormer windows are now reduced by the roof lowering. The easternmost of the two small northern projections houses a secondary turnpike stair.

The basement is divided into two chambers, one twice the size of the other though very ill-lit. Neither are vaulted. The smaller room has two windows and is separated from the other by a sort of pend.

The upper floor is undivided and forms a lengthy gallery of fully 63 feet, with staircases to north and south, and communicating on the west with the earlier 16th century part of the castle. It would be interesting to know for what purpose this handsome gallery was built, probably in 1632. Its eastern window is very

[20]

large for the period, and carries a fine pediment above its pilasters, inscribed E.W.M. for William, 7th Earl of Morton. On a corner of the south wing is a sundial bearing the initials of the same Earl and his Countess. He lived from 1606 to 1648, and was an important man of his day.

There is a 17th century Renaissance gateway to the castle, guarded by gunloops. The property happily is now cared for by the Ministry of Works.

In 1458 James Douglas of Dalkeith was created Lord Aberdour and Earl of Morton. His male line failed three generations later when an heiress carried title and property to another branch of the family. She married James, only a younger son of Sir George Douglas of Pittendreich, yet in right of his wife he became 4th Earl of Morton. He it was who developed into the infamous Chancellor and later Regent Morton, dictator of Scotland, hater of Mary Queen of Scots, murderer of Darnley, one of the most violent men of a violent age, who profited more than any other out of the Scottish Reformation. In his day Aberdour Castle must have witnessed many a savage and stirring scene.

THE MANSE, ANSTRUTHER EASTER

This interesting and attractive house must be almost unique in that, though seemingly an entirely typical laird's fortalice of the late 16th century, it was in fact built as a manse. Its erector was the well-known autobiographer, Master James Melville, minister of the parish of Kilrenny, whose autobiography is recognised by historians to be a most valuable account of the state of Scotland in the stirring times of James Sixth's reign. As well as being a literary man, Master Melville appears to have been a man of some means, for he paid for the building himself, in the end, although he observes that the parish 'oblesit thamselves to big me a hous upon a piece of ground quhilk the Lard of Anstruther gaiff frielie for that effect'. It cost him more than 3,500 merks—the parish only contributing 'about 3,000 sleds of stones and 14 or 15 chalders of lime'. The Melvilles, of course, were powerful folk in the newly Reformed Kirk, and they were also a most prominent Fife family.

The builder's own account of the work is worth quoting, in part.

'This was undertakin and begoun at Whitsonday in an.1590 but would never haiff bein perfyted giff the bountifull hand of my God haid nocht maid me to tak the wark in hand myselff, and furnished stranglie to my consideration all things neidfull, sa that never ouk (week) passed but all sort of workmen was weill peyit, never a dayes intermission fra the beginning to the compleitting of it, and never a soar fingar during the haill labour. In Junie begoun and in the monethe of Merch efter I was resident therin . . . thairfor justlie I may call it a spectakle of God's liberalitie.'

The house was originally built on the L-plan but the main block was extended in the 17th century, making it approximate to the letter T, with a narrow corbelled-out stair-turret rising in the re-entrant. The main block is of three storeys, the roof level having been somewhat raised, so that the stair-tower and turret would originally have seemed taller. This is a storey higher than the rest, and is notable for its two upper storeys projecting slightly on a continuous corbel-course. On the gable of this is a stone panel bearing, not the usual coat-of-arms but the words 'THE WATCH TOWER'.

[22]

The doorway is in the usual place at the foot of the stair-wing, and gives access to the three vaulted chambers of the main block and the one unvaulted of the 17th-century extension. The main wide turnpike stair rises only to the first floor, above which the ascent was continued by the turret-stair, which is now removed.

The walls are harled, with dressed stone margins to the windows, some of which have been enlarged. There is a 17th-century dovecot in the garden.

Ephraim Melville, son of the builder, sold the house, which had become, of course, his own property, to the neighbouring Laird of Anstruther of that Ilk, and it was occupied by that family for some time. When the new mansion of Anstruther Place was built in 1663, this old manse became the dower-house. In 1713 however Sir John Anstruther made exchange of it with Anstruther Town Council for another house in the burgh, and this fine building once more became the parish minister's manse.

AIRDRIE HOUSE

This is a plain old house with an interesting and unusual stair-wing feature, standing approximately three miles west of Crail. It consists of a long and entirely plain main block, the windows of which have been enlarged and which has seen considerable other alteration over the years, with the short square wing projecting to the south, dating from the late 16th century. This wing rises a storey higher than the main house, being slightly offset above first and second floor levels, the present hipped roof being an obvious alteration. This wing formerly contained a squared scale-and-platt stair to the first floor, from the entrance which lies in the foot of it, above which the ascent was, and is, continued via the turret stair corbelled out in the re-entrant, partly supported on a squinch—as at nearby Kellie Castle. The upper portion of this turret is unusual, rising above the present roof level to end in a parapeted look-out platform with small dummy open rounds. This platform is reached by still another tiny stair-turret ending in a stone-roofed caphouse. The parapet is ashlar-built and pierced by quatrefoil gunloops.

A window linel bears a monogram, apparently M.C.L.O.A., presumably referring to a Magister C. Lumsdaine of Airdrie. Another small ornamented panel-space is dated 1588, which well suits the style of the tower.

Airdrie was a barony of the Lumsdaines or Lumsdens, a well-known Fife family as early as 1450. It later passed into the possessions of the Prestons, Anstruthers and Erskines.

BALMUTO HOUSE

The ancient home of the Boswells has fallen on sad days. Indeed, the old tower may be no more when this is printed, the rest of the house having been already demolished around it.

The sketch shows the original 15th century keep, square, plain but sturdy, with ornamental windows inserted later. If this tower survives it will be thanks to the problem of pulling down its six-foot thick walls.

These walls are of fine worked stone, and the crenellated parapet is notable in being projected on single corbels each carved to a simple design. There are no rounds at the angles. Roof and walk are drained not by the usual array of cannon-like spouts, but by single larger lip-like projections in the centre of each wall. The present roof is flat, but may once have been gabled within the parapet.

The enlarged decorative windows date, on the north side, which was always exposed, from 1680; but on the south, formerly covered by later work, they appear to be earlier by at least a century. The basement is vaulted. There appears to have been a service hatch of sorts down from the Hall on the first floor, in the ingoing of the south window. The turnpike stair has risen in the south-west angle.

The fifth Boswell in Balmuto got many properties erected into a barony by 1477, and it was probably then that the tower was built. The family retained possession until modern times.

BALCOMIE CASTLE

Seen from afar off, rising high out of its sheltering trees, the tall old tower of Balcomie is still impressive although today merely attached to a farmhouse and only a fragment of a once extensive castle of the second half of the 16th century. It stands above the shore at Fife Ness, the very eastern extremity of the county, about two miles from Crail.

The present building consists of a lofty L-shaped tower, five storeys and a garret in height, but even so with a lowered roof-line. The wing is joined to the main block at an angle, to form two re-entrants, and in the southern of these a small stair-turret is corbelled out between first and second floor levels only, provided with a shot-hole. Two truncated two-storeyed angle-turrets, now with oversailing roofs, crown the gable of the wing. These are pierced with shot-holes, both round and quatrefoil, as are other parts of the walling. Most of the windows, which have good moulded surrounds, have been built up. The masonry is of very fine coursed rubble, with the turrets of ashlar. The basement is vaulted. The original main stair was a turnpike rising in a circular tower projecting from the north end of the main block, the entrance being at the foot thereof.

The castle in its heyday extended to the east and north-east of this building, to form two sides of a large courtyard, which was walled-in elsewhere. The fragmentary vaulting and foundations of these substantial additions are still evident, but lack of space forbids any description of these here. In the centre of the south range however, is a fine arched pend and gatehouse above, the latter unfortunately much altered and given a modern roof. This gatehouse has been flanked by vaulted chambers, guardroom and porter's room, and protected by gunloops. Three armorial panels surmount the archway, displaying the arms of Learmonth and Myrton of Randerston, with the mottoes SANS FEINTISE and ADVYSEDLIE, with the date 1602. Above is the inscription THE LORD BVILD THE HOVSE THEY LABOUR IN VAINE THAT BVILD IT.

Apparently a John de Balcomie was in possession of this property in 1375, but nothing of the present structure dates from so early a period. We find Balcomie being granted by James Fifth to James Learmonth of Clatto in 1526, with authority to build a fortalice. A charter of 1537, however, confirmed therein another Learmonth, Sir James of Dairsie, who had bought the lands. Which of these built the original castle is not clear; possibly both were involved. At anyrate, the house was sufficiently constructed in 1538 to give hospitality and shelter to Mary of Guise on her first landing in Scotland to meet her husband to be. Fife Ness seems a strange spot for the new queen to land, and it seems stranger still that James Fifth did not come to meet her there but awaited her presentation to him by Learmonth at St. Andrews. This Sir James was twice ambassador to England, and fell at the Battle of Pinkie.

Additions were made to Balcomie later in the 16th century, and in the early 17th, as well as in more modern times. Sir James Learmonth of Balcomie perished in 1598 in the ill-fated and unhappy Fife Adventurers expedition to the Lewis, and the estate passed to his brother, Sir John, of Birkhill, who presumably built the gatehouse. His son, another Sir James, was President of the Court of Session, and his grandson, dying without issue, Balcomie passed to a nephew, son of Sir William Gordon of Lesmoir, Solicitor to James Seventh. Later it was held by Sir William Hope, Scott of Scotstarvit, and the Earl of Kellie—the latter being responsible for reducing it to its present size.

It is said that James Fourth intended forming a royal demesne at Balcomie, and had acquired the lands when his death at Flodden intervened.

BALGONIE CASTLE

Unfortunately this very fine example of a 15th-century tower-house, set in an early 17th-century enclosure, is in a poor state of repair and decaying further. The later outbuildings have long been ruinous, but the free-standing 15th-century keep itself remains externally complete, although the roof is now collapsing. It is situated about a mile south-east of Markinch, on the steep bank of the River Leven. It will be sad indeed if it is allowed to moulder away.

The tower, built of good ashlar, rises four storeys to a parapet, with garret above. The battlements and parapet appear to have been renewed in the 16th century. The unusually wide parapet-walk is provided with the usual open rounds at all angles save the north-east, where the stairway rises to end in a look-out chamber with gunloop.

Both ground and first floor chambers are vaulted, and were entered by separate outside doors, both in the east front, the upper one originally reached by a removable wooden stair. The lower vault has only narrow slits for light, and no fireplace, and could have been used as a prison or for storage. The Hall, on the first floor, has no actual fireplace either, the position of an open hearth being shown by two outlets for smoke formed in the gables—a most unusual and primitive arrangement.

The stair rises within the thickness of the north-east angle. The second floor apartment has a large fireplace which has been reduced in size in the 17th century, windows with stone seats, and a mural closet with external projection for sanitary convenience. It would look, therefore, as though this was the lord's own living-quarters, and the smoky Hall below in this instance only for his henchmen. The third floor is of similar arrangement. Over the garret floor fireplace is a damaged armorial panel in plaster, of 17th-century date. The parapet-walk is drained by elaborate cannon-like spouts, alternately octagonal and twisted.

Additions were made to the south and east, to form a courtyard, in the late 15th, 16th and 17th centuries. Access to the earliest of these additions was originally gained by a wooden bridge from the tower—as at Huntingtower in Perthshire—thus avoiding blocking the original entrances and adding to security. In a building in the enclosure is a panel, with the initials F.S.A.L.

[28]

and D.A.R. for Field Marshall Sir Alexander Leslie and his wife Dame Agnes Renton. The Field Marshall, famous Scottish soldier, was in 1641 created Lord Balgonie and first Earl of Leven.

The original tower was probably built by Sir John Sibbald. His daughter and heiress married Sir Robert Lundie, who became Lord High Treasurer. Their eldest son was Sheriff of Fife. The Lundie family retained possession until 1640 when Leslie acquired it, and made several additions. It was thereafter held by successive Earls of Leven. During the Jacobite Rising of 1715 it was garrisoned by the Hanoverians under General Cadogan, who eventually became Government Commander-in-Chief. The famous Rob Roy MacGregor with 200 clansmen marched here from Falkland, which he had already taken, and besieged and successfully took Balgonie, partly dismantling it.

In 1824 the estate was sold to James Balfour of Whittinghame, of the family of A. J. Balfour the Prime Minister, for the vast sum of £104,000. It is said that the new purchaser intended to restore the castle and make it habitable again. Unfortunately this was never done, and the impressive fortalice appears only too likely to become one more casualty of time and neglect.

COLLAIRNIE CASTLE

This most interesting relic of a former extensive 16th-century castle dominates the farm-toun of Collairnie, in the North Fife valley between Dunbog Hill and Norman's Law, about four miles east of Newburgh. The site, though not now having any aspect of strength, may have once been surrounded by marshland. It has been a large and impressive building, L-shaped on plan with enclosing curtain walling. Unfortunately it has fallen on evil days, and has been incorporated into the modern farm-steading, the main block reduced to a single storey, the remaining tower roof slightly lowered so as to over-sail the turrets, and other indignities perpetrated upon it.

The remaining portions are the tall wing of four storeys and a garret, with a semi-circular stair-tower in the former re-entrant angle. This wing appears always to have been a storey higher than the main block, traces of the masonry of the latter still remaining. The walls are of rubble, and appear to date from the second half of the 16th century—though it is possible that the reduced main block may have contained still older work. Angle turrets crown the two former external angles of the tower, which is well-provided with gunloops. Many of the windows have been built up, and have had boldly moulded surrounds. A cannon-shaped spout projects at eaves level on the north front, to carry off rainwater from the former main-block roof. There is a good cable moulding at first floor level on the south or re-entrant front, and there have been the usual dormer windows at attic level, now no more owing to the lowering of the roof.

There are two entrances, both at the foot of the stair-tower, one admitting to the ground floor and the other to the foot of the stair, there being no connection at this level. The basement is divided into two cellars, only one of which is vaulted, curiously enough. The stair is also unusual in that its turnpike turns in an anti-clockwise direction—possibly as a defensive measure. Probably, like the Border Kerrs, its builder was left-handed, or 'kerry-pawed'. The first floor has been remodelled in the 18th century, and has been pine-panelled.

Above are the principal attractions of Collairnie—the very fine tempera painted ceilings of the second and third floor chambers. These have been a magnificent feature, comprising much floral and scroll work, wise saws, and the heraldry of over fifty famous Scots families, mainly of Fife. One of the legends declares: FLIE YE COMPENY OF A LIER. BUT THOW MUST NEIDES KEIP COMPENY WT HIM. BEWAR YAT IN NA WAYES THOW TROW HIM.

The heraldry shows, amongst the others, a number of Balfour coats, named as such—more than the Barclay shields. This, together with the fact that both names have the initial B, seems to have given rise to confusion on the part of historical writers as to whether it was Barclays or Balfours who built Collairnie. This is quite unnecessary. The Barclays were lairds of Collairnie from the 14th century until 1717, when the line ended in an heiress; and even then, her successors adopted the name of Steuart-Barclay of Collairnie. Inter-marriage with the great Fife family of Balfour, and the fact that in 1789 the property was sold to a son of Balfour of Fernie, has added to the confusion.

It is believed that Mary Queen of Scots spent three days at Collairnie on her way to meet Darnley at St. Andrews in 1564. The son of the laird of her time, David Barclay, was given the custody here of a notorious Border riever, Ringan Armstrong, captured in some foray, and held responsible for his security on a bond of £2,000. This laird's initials D.B. and those of his wife M.W. dated 1581 appear on the lintel of the door to the basement, below a panel space, which at a later date has been filled with a triangular pediment, probably from a dormer, bearing the Balfour arms, and the initials H.B., dated 1607 —causing further confusion as to lairdship. This seems to refer to Helen Balfour, wife of the next laird, another David Barclay, who succeeded in 1587. This laird was concerned, with the Earl of Bothwell in an attempt to kidnap King James Sixth at Holyroodhouse in 1592.

THE ABBOT'S HOUSE, DUNFERMLINE

This house, now forming part of the Dunfermline streets of Abbot Street and Maygate, should more properly be called the Commendator's House, for it was built after the Reformation in the late 16th century, as the laird's house of the wealthy secularised lordship of Dunfermline Abbey, the richest plum of all the choice church lands of Scotland. It was never the house of the true abbot.

The building, which had been divided into two houses for some time, is now in process of renovation. Originally it was a single commodious fortalice consisting of a long oblong main block, two storeys and an attic in height, with a stair-tower near the centre of the north front, and another, seen in sketch, projecting southwards at the east end. Stair-turrets are corbelled out in the re-entrants of each, to give access to watch-chambers in the upper storeys of the towers, that to the south being the larger. To the north, there has been considerable alteration, in the late 17th century, and the space flanking that stair-tower on either side has been filled in, and another doorway formed. A large addition was also made at the eastern gable.

The south front is more or less unaltered, though most of the windows have been enlarged and some filled up, as has a doorway in the re-entrant. The attic dormer windows have triangular pediments. There is an alcove at ground level in the centre of this south front, for purposes unknown. A shot-hole opens at second floor level in the east side of the north stair-tower, and another is said to have been placed on the west wall of the south tower.

Internally there have been many and drastic alterations. The basement contained four vaulted chambers, but the vault of one of these has been removed at an early date.

The lands and properties of Dunfermline Abbey, being the richest in the kingdom, were considered the greatest prize for the land-hungry nobles of the post-Reformation period, and they passed from one to another in an unscrupulous game of grab. The first Reformed Commendator was one Robert Pitcairn, and he it was who presumably built this house, for few of the other and more lofty holders retained possession for long enough to do much building—and anyway, had large castles elsewhere. Captain

James Stewart, Earl of Arran, held the lands for a short time during his Chancellorship, but the talented and unscrupulous Master of Gray, who had worked with him, managed to gain them from him as the price of effecting Arran's escape from a disaster that the Master himself had engineered. Three years later, however, Gray likewise had to part with them as the price of the Earl of Huntly's assistance in saving him from a well-merited sentence of hanging for high treason. Huntly, ever in Catholic revolt, had Dunfermline taken from him by King James himself, and bestowed on his fifteen-year-old Queen, Anne of Denmark, as a belated wedding-gift—James himself of course drawing the revenues. Anne evidently did not find the Commendator's House adequate for a royal residence, and she built her own much larger house nearby, which has been called the Queen's House, or Anne of Denmark's Building, and which has now been demolished. Anne appointed Alexander Seton, later Chancellor of Scotland and Earl of Dunfermline, to the hereditary bailieship of the Abbey lands in 1593.

EARLSHALL

This is one of the most interesting and unusual fortalices in a county rich in such buildings. It stands about a mile east of Leuchars in country that was anciently forest. The house dates from various periods in the 16th and 17th centuries, and had fallen into near ruin until most admirably restored by the late Sir Robert Lorimer in 1892.

The castle has originally formed four sides of a courtyard, the main house (as seen in sketch) making up two sides, with a secondary detached tower, and a lower range of 17th-century out-buildings. The entrance to this courtyard is by an archway provided with a battlemented projection above and a gunloop at the side. Over it is a panel bearing the arms of Sir William Bruce, the builder.

The principal building is a development of the L-plan, consisting of a main block of three storeys and a garret, plus a wing slightly higher, having in the angle between them a rounded stair-tower corbelled out to the square at the top to form a parapeted watch-platform. More unusual is the large oval tower, containing small rooms on each floor, at the other corner of the main block. I have never come across another tower quite like this. It has a tiny stair-turret projecting between it and the main gable. The main block attic windows have dormer pediments bearing the initials W.B. and D.A.L. and heraldic carvings.

The door is at the foot of the round stair-tower, as is usual, with more armorial panels above. The ground floor chambers are vaulted. The Hall is on the first floor, a handsome room with a fireplace 9 feet wide, heraldically decorated. The walls are pine-panelled.

The second floor contains a splendid gallery, 50 by 18 feet, with a remarkable wooden ceiling, painted in tempera with heraldry, animals and proverbs, and dated 1620. A sense of humour has been at work here, for as well as the arms of famous Fife families with which the Bruces inter-married, and other Scottish coats, there are also fanciful escutcheons accredited to such as King David of Israel, Joshua, Julius Caesar and so on. The animals include such exotic creatures as a coatimondi from Brazil, a dromedary, an ostrich, an Arabian mouse and an armadillo. Also there are verses, such as: 'A NICE WYF AND A

BACK DOORE OFT MAKETH A RICH MAN POORE'; and 'BE MERRYE AND GLAD, HONEST AND VERTUOVS, FOR THAR SVFFICETH THE ANGER OF THE INVYOVS.' In Latin, is the inscription declaring that William Bruce began to build this house in 1546; it was completed by his great-grandson William Bruce in 1617.

The smaller detached tower nearby is also L-shaped and rises to three storeys the lower two of which are vaulted.

The property, formerly called Leuchars-Monypenny, came to Alexander Bruce of the family of Clackmannan towards the end of the 15th century. His son, the Sir William who began the building of the present house, was an extraordinary man who lived almost a century, fought at Flodden with James Fourth, escaped, and yet lived to see the great-grandson of that monarch, James Sixth, acknowledged as heir to the throne of the United Kingdom. His son having died in the meantime, he was succeeded by his grandson Alexander, who also did some building; it was the great grandson, however, another Sir William who added all the magnificent decoration. He died in 1636, and his son was killed at the Battle of Worcester, fighting for King Charles. The next Bruce was less heroic, being one of the most notorious persecutors of the Covenanters during the 'killing times'. He is said to have paid one guinea for the satisfaction of hacking off the head and hands of the martyred divine Richard Cameron—and sold the trophies for £500.

The property later passed to the Hendersons of Fordell.

FERNIE CASTLE

This most handsome and interesting mansion stands in rural surroundings about four miles west of Cupar, and may be seen from the public road (B.937). It is a tall 16th-century tower on the L-plan, to which considerable additions have been made in the late 17th century and later, the walls harled and yellow-washed. Fortunately the original fortalice is clearly to be distinguished. The site has formerly been a strong one, protected by a marsh.

The tower lies to the west, and consists of a main block of four storeys with a stair-wing extending southwards a storey higher, to contain a tiny watch-chamber, and another circular tower projecting at an angle to the north-west, this being corbelled out to the square at the top to contain another watch-chamber. This latter is served by a tiny turret-stair in the western re-entrant. This constitutes a distinctly unusual development of the traditional L-plan, not quite a T. Many of the windows have been enlarged, but certain of the defensive slit variety survive. A cannon-type spout projects just below the eaves at the west end, to carry off rain-water from the joining of the roofs of tower and main block.

The original door, which was in the main re-entrant angle, has been transformed into a window, and the entrance is now further east in the later extension. Near the original door the wide turnpike stair rises in the wing. The ground floor is vaulted, but the interior has been largely modernised. The round tower with the tall conical roof, to the north-east, is not original work.

The history of Fernie is confusing to unravel, the barony having been divided as early as the 14th century into Easter and Wester, and both sections eventually held by branches of the Balfour family. However this, Wester Fernie, seems always to have been the principal property. Originally the lands were part of the domains of the MacDuff Earls of Fife, but by the 15th century Wester Fernie was held by a family known as Fernie of that Ilk. Whether the Fernies built the original portion of the present house is not clear, for the Fernie line failed in an heiress who married a Lovell of Balumbie, whereafter the lands were sold to a cadet of Arnot of that Ilk in 1580. The style of architecture might well indicate him to be the builder: on the other hand, the little cross which very unusually crowns the gable of the stair-wing, might well indicate a pre-Reformation date of erection in the early 16th century, when the Fernies would still be in possession. The Arnots retained the property for about a century until, again through lack of a direct heir, Fernie went to the third Lord Balfour of Burleigh, a far-away connection. He gave the property to his second son, Colonel John Balfour, who like his nephew, the Master of Burleigh, was attainted for his share in the Rising of 1715, and his estates forfeited. His elder brother, Arthur was however an officer on the Hanoverian side —a precaution not so very unusual in those troubled times—and King George granted him his brother's lands in 1720. One of the later Fernie lairds, Major Francis Balfour, laid claim to the dormant and forfeited peerage of Balfour of Burleigh in 1869, but it was adjudged by the House of Lords to go to Alexander Bruce of Kennet, who succeeded in the female line, under a special clause in the original grant of the title.

The duties of Forester of Falkland and Constable of Cupar were associated with the lairdship of Fernie.

FORDELL CASTLE

This excellent example of a late 16th-century fortalice stands within a large estate and walled garden about three miles west of Aberdour. It was superceded by a modern mansionhouse, but has been restored and is maintained in good condition.

It consists of an oblong main block running east and west with square towers at the north-west and south-east angles, these being stair-wings. The walls rise to three storeys and an attic, with the towers a storey higher containing small chambers reached by turret-stairs. That to the south-east has a gabled roof, while that to the north-west is finished with a flat roof and parapet —as in sketch. The masonry is coursed rubble, there are angle-turrets corbelled out at opposite angles to the towers, and only on the south side are the attic windows dormers, with worn carved pediments.

The entrance is in the foot of the north stair-tower. It gives access to a vaulted corridor running along the north front, from which the three vaulted basement chambers are entered. The eastermost was the kitchen, which could also be reached from the foot of the south-east tower. From the west chamber a small spiral stair rises in the thickness of the wall to the Hall above.

The first and second floors have been much altered, the second floor having been removed and a gallery installed. The first floor contained the Hall to the west and a smaller withdrawing-room to the east. The north-west stair rises only to this level, above which the ascent is continued by the turret stair. This gives access to a rather remarkable chamber directly above the main stair-head, known as Queen Mary's Room. This is vaulted and panelled. Three steps higher is the main third floor, containing two rooms, formerly panelled, from which open tiny chambers in the angle-turrets, these latter projecting inwards slightly. They have small windows with shot-holes below. The stair in the south tower rises a storey higher than the other. Both towers have a watch-chamber above main third floor level, that to the north, above Queen Mary's Room, also being vaulted, to support the flat stone roof within the parapet.

The lintel of the door in the north tower is inscribed I.H. (for James Henderson the builder) 25 MCH. A.D. 1580. Higher is built in a broken lintel, also inscribed I.H. and also I.M. (for Jean

Murray of Tullibardine, his wife) dated 1580. There is a heraldic panel with the Henderson and Murray arms, above.

Altogether the house is a delightful one. Fordell was acquired by James Henrisoun or Henderson, Lord Justice Clerk, about 1511, and the family has long been prominent in Fife. They had an attractive town-house in nearby Inverkeithing, of slightly later date, which is still extant. The family, which derived from Dumfriesshire, claim as a cadet Alexander Henderson, one of the leaders of the Reformation.

GRANGE

This pleasant farmhouse incorporates all that remains of the mansion of the famous William Kirkcaldy of Grange, whose valiant efforts on behalf of Mary Queen of Scots are well-known, and who was shamefully executed by the Regent Morton after surrendering on terms Edinburgh Castle of which he was Governor. Morton thereafter bestowed Grange on his own illegitimate son. Kirkcaldy's father, Sir James, Lord High Treasurer to James Fifth and to Queen Mary, had had the lands, tower and fortalice of Grange erected into a free barony in 1540.

The round tower, with its interesting stringcourses and gun-loop appears to date from the 16th century, as may well part of the main block of the present farmhouse. The gable to the left of the sketch is modern, as is the doorway in the foot of the tower. A doorway, formerly external but now enclosed by modern work on the north side of the main block, bears an inscribed lintel dated 1687 and the monogram I S M.

Internally there have been great alterations. The basement is not now evidently vaulted, but as the ceiling is extremely low and the flooring of the first storey was of stone within living memory, there may have been vaulting. The tower probably once housed a stair.

The house is in excellent condition and well cared for. There are portions of a fine old garden wall remaining.

WORMISTONE HOUSE

Within a copse of wind-blown trees only a couple of miles from Fife Ness, and not far from Balcomie Castle, stands the small early 17th-century house of Wormistone, much added to and altered in later times. The nucleus is a three-storeyed L-shaped building, with a stair-turret corbelled out above first floor level in the re-entrant angle, the walls harled and whitewashed. Unfortunately the roof level has been altered, presumably lowered, to the detriment of the general appearance, and the pediments of the displaced dormer windows inserted elsewhere in the walling. Two of these have Latin inscriptions, one being dated 1612. Another bears a worn coat-of-arms that may represent Balfour. Other windows have been enlarged, and the turret-roof has been heightened out of proportion. The trefoil-shaped shot-hole in the turret does not appear to be original, any more than is the long slit-window above. The building is not now in the best of condition.

The property was long a possession of the family of Spens of Wormistone, Constables of Crail. In 1612 it passed to the Balfours, who were everywhere in Fife expanding at this period, and who probably built the present nucleus. Nine years later, however, Patrick Lindsay was the laird, and this family retained possession until comparatively modern times. They succeeded eventually to the Earldom of Lindsay, the seat of which is at Kilconquhar House some ten miles distant.

HILL HOUSE, DUNFERMLINE

This is rather a remarkable house, with two faces. Standing on the crest of a small hill, about one mile south of the centre of Dunfermline, it is a tall L-planned fortalice, and from north, east and south appears to be a very typical example of its kind, stern, plain and uncompromising, rubble-built and without ornamentation. Then, round to the west where the angle of the L opens, we gain a vastly different impression. Here is quite a pretentious mansion. The stonework is carefully wrought ashlar, not rubble; the windows are larger, with moulded jambs and surmounted by decorative pediments; stringcourses adorn the walling; there are heraldic and inscribed panels; and a semi-hexagonal stair-tower rises in the re-entrant to finish in an extraordinary parapet, consisting of a balustrade formed out of great pierced stone letters, which read NI DEVS AEDIFICET DOMVN (Except the Lord build the house). I have never seen another like this—nor indeed another house with two such contrasting aspects.

The building is unusual, also, in having a small square tower projecting eastwards from the wing of the L. This tower, tall and offset on corbelling, looks as though it should contain another stair, but does not. It appears to date from the late 16th century, rather earlier than the remainder of the house, and may well represent all that remains of a previous fortalice on the site. As a whole, Hill House dates from the 17th century.

The original doorway was in the south wall of the hexagonal stair-tower, but this has been covered over by a modern single-storey building in the re-entrant angle. Above the former door-way is a scrolled panel dated 1623, with the inscription, in Hebrew and Latin 'Woe Unto Him That Hath Builded His House By Unrighteousness'. Elsewhere on the stair-tower is an empty panel-space, and over windows are pediments showing a seated figure playing a harp, and a bearded man in 17th-century costume, with an open book. A third pediment contains a heraldic cartouche showing three buckles, and the initials W.M., for William Monteith. Two long chimney-stacks rising above the flat roof of the stair-tower are linked by a panel, with another Hebrew and Latin quotation declaring 'This Also is Vanity and a Great Evil'. It is perhaps not surprising to learn that the 17th-century builder, William Monteith of Randieford, who acquired Hill House in 1621, was a pious elder of the Kirk.

The house has been much modernised internally, but certain interesting features remain. The ground floor is not vaulted, but the kitchen in the east gable retains its wide arched fireplace. In the course of a restoration some years ago, certain fireplaces were brought from Culross and inserted here by the proprietor, one in the drawing-room being very handsomely carved and dated 1661. The wide principal turnpike stair rises only to second floor level, above which the ascent to the attic floor and the small rooms at the head of both the east and stair towers is continued by a little stair contrived in the walling, an unusual arrangement.

This most interesting house, now the property of the Earl of Elgin, is occupied by appreciative tenants and maintained in good order.

KELLIE CASTLE

Standing on the south side of Kellie Law, three miles north of St. Monans, this most impressive house, though now occupied and in good order, was all but a roofless ruin when Professor James Lorimer took it over and restored it in 1878.

The building approximates to the letter T on plan, but this is the result of development. It consists of a three-storey main block with three large square towers, two forming the cross-pieces of the T, at the west end, and the third at the bottom of the leg. There are also two smaller stair-towers projecting from the north front (not seen in sketch). The main towers rise to five storeys, those at the north-west and south-west being embellished with typical late-16th-century angle-turrets. A stair-turret is also corbelled out in the re-entrant of south-west tower and main block, supported on a squinch. Another squinch supports the corbelling of another smaller stair-turret on the north side of the east tower. These squinches are a rather uncommon device. There is one at nearby Airdrie House.

The oldest part of the house is undoubtedly the north-west tower, the masonry here being notably more rough and massive. It seems likely that the original house consisted of a simple square tower here, with curtain walling enclosing a fair-sized courtyard—a typical 15th- or early 16th-century arrangement. This was added to in the late 16th century by increasing the height of the tower and building new work, using the existing curtain walling as part thereof. The east tower has the date 1573 inscribed high on its south wall. Then, in 1606 the large south-west tower was added and what is now the main block built to link up with the east tower. This date appears on one of the dormer windows here. This seems the most probable development of the present large and complicated house.

The entire ground floor is vaulted, with the kitchen to the right in the main block. A handsome squared stair rises from the main doorway in the foot of the south-west tower only as far as the first floor, whereafter the ascent is continued by no fewer than four different turnpike stairs. The Hall, on the first floor, is a fine chamber, 50 feet long by 21 feet wide.

Kellie was held by the family of Oliphant from 1360 until 1613, when, through the extravagance of the 5th Lord Oliphant it was sold to Sir Thomas Erskine, created Viscount Fentoun and later first Earl of Kellie, one of James Sixth's prime favourites, who was closely concerned with that monarch in the unsavoury business of the Gowrie Conspiracy, and actually slew Alexander Ruthven, the Earl of Gowrie's brother, in Gowrie House. His descendants retained possession until the death of the tenth Earl in 1829, when the title merged with the Earldom of Mar, and the house was allowed to sink into ruin.

The actual building, therefore, seems to be all the work of the Oliphants, but much of the internal decoration, including some excellent 17th-century ceilings in the Hall and other public rooms, was the work of the 3rd and 4th Earls of Kellie, some of it dated 1674.

All praise to Professor Lorimer for saving this handsome and interesting relic of an older and prouder Scotland, which is still occupied by his descendants.

KILCONQUHAR HOUSE

The large mansion of Kilconquhar stands within its estate close to the village, two miles north of Elie. Although mainly a modern structure, it clusters round a tall L-shaped tower of the 16th century, which only from the west may be viewed clearly from ground to roofline. It is rubble-built and five storeys in height, with angle-turrets of ashlar at all corners. The original stair-tower in the re-entrant has been removed, but replaced by another in the 18th century, in the same position; the additional turret-stair of the former, rising from the fourth floor to the flat roof, still adjoins. The upper storey of the wing overhangs slightly on a stringcourse. All windows save those of the turrets have been enlarged.

Sir John Bellenden, Lord Justice Clerk in the second half of the 16th century, may have been the builder. He was much involved in the intrigues of the Court of the young King James Sixth. He worked in close harness with the notorious Master of Gray in the matter of pulling down the Chancellor, the Earl of Arran. Bellenden in fact assured Elizabeth's ambassador, Wotton, that he would find an assassin for Arran if he would engage that his royal mistress would protect him thereafter. Curiously enough, the proposed murderer was Douglas, Provost of Lincluden Abbey.

This enterprising Lord Justice Clerk left many estates, and Kilconquhar went to his eldest son by his third wife. Later it passed to the Lindsay family, the present laird being the Earl of Lindsay.

MONIMAIL TOWER

This small tower is all that remains of the former great palace of the Archbishops of St. Andrews. It is an interesting fragment, however, of superior workmanship, as is to be expected. It stands amongst the gardens of Melville House, and was obviously the flanking tower of a large courtyard-type castle.

The building is square and rises to four storeys, with a flat roof within a non-crenellated parapet. Probably this roof was originally gabled in the usual manner; the stairway ends in a little caphouse with pyramidal roof which has been reduced in height, so clearly there have been alterations at this level. The walls are of good coursed rubble with dressed facings, the parapet being all of ashlar. It has open rounds at the angles, and is pierced by small shot-holes. Stringcourses enhance the north and west sides; elsewhere there would be adjoining wings. Also at parapet level are decorative roundels containing carved heads, similar to those at Stirling Castle and Falkland Palace, typical of 'official' 16th-century architecture. Others contain the arms of Bethune, or Beaton, of Balfour, and of Balfour of Pittendreich.

The notorious Cardinal Beaton is said to have built this tower, and the lower part may be his work, but the upper levels are of later construction and post-Reformation alteration, dated 1578. There was an episcopal residence here reputedly as early as 1300, however.

After the Reformation, the lands of the sacked palace passed to the Balfours, and thence to the Melvilles.

MYRES CASTLE

Although its situation in low-lying ground just south of Auchter-muchty gives no impression of strength, the name of this most attractive fortalice reveals that formerly it stood in the midst of a mire or marsh, which would serve very well for defensive purposes. It is now a rambling house dating from various periods and difficult to describe briefly. The original building seems to have consisted of two blocks or wings joined at their angles, each having a round tower projecting from diagonally opposite corners. That to the north has been greatly hedged about and altered by later extensions, but the southern section and probably the earliest (as seen in sketch) remains fairly distinct, although the upper portion of the circular tower has been transformed in the early 17th century, and the roof-line of the main block altered still later.

To deal with the most prominent feature first—the south-east circular tower has been built out to the square and raised an extra storey to finish in a flat roof within a parapet. This upper storey and parapet-walk are served by a little stair in a corbelled-out turret in the angle, finishing in a conical-roofed caphouse—all a very attractive composition. This extension is of good worked stone, or ashlar, the remainder of the house being rubble-built and harled. The parapet itself is enhanced by two panels within garlands, bearing the arms of Paterson and Mure, the initials s.p. and e.m., and the date 1616. It was a late period to be building parapets.

The main portion of the building is said to have arisen around a nucleus of 1490, but later additions, window enlargements and so on give a generally late-17th-century impression. There are, however, a number of gunloops of both the oval splayed and circular varieties.

Internally there has been much modernisation, inevitably, but many interesting features survive. The ground floor is vaulted. The basement of the south-east round tower contains two tiers of gunloops, the lower oval and the upper rectangular, the last having been reached by a timber staging—which gives the impression that this part of the fortalice at least was designed for serious defence. The Hall is on the first floor, as usual, with a private room opening off, it having a little stair leading down to

[48]

the vaulted cellar below—no doubt a private access to the laird's locked wine-cellar. There is domestic accommodation above.

Historically also the Myres of Auchtermuchty is interesting. When James First was held prisoner in England he became so attached to his young English page Robert Coxwell that he brought him with him on his return to Scotland, and gave him the major portion of the royal property of Auchtermuchty, including the Myres, plus a pension of 20 merks. When Coxwell died in 1453 he left Myres to his widow, who married John Scrymgeour, second son of the Constable of Dundee. He held the office of Claviger, or mace-bearer to the King, and by some peculiar arrangement the office thereafter went with the ownership of the lands of Myres. This new laird probably built the nucleus of the present house. Another John Scrymgeour, Master of the King's Works, was laird and Claviger in 1531. Myres remained with the Scrymgeours until the 17th century, when we find John Paterson served heir of his father Michael Paterson of the Myres in 1628, and in the office of Claviger, with the sum of ten guineas as well as feus of the lands as annual fee for the said office. The S.P. initials of the heraldic panel on the south-east tower was for Stephen Paterson who married Elizabeth Mure.

This delightful house, in its remarkable clipped-yew gardens, is still occupied and in good repair.

PITCAIRLIE HOUSE

Standing within its estate, at the very north-western extremity of the county, near the Perthshire border, two miles south of Newburgh, Pitcairlie is in the main an 18th-century mansion which was again altered about 1800. But there is a considerable nucleus of the 16th century, and the tower projecting at the southern angle is wholly of that period—these remaining 16th-century portions having a distinct resemblance to those at Myres Castle near Auchtermuchty, not very far away. It is now difficult to decide upon the original plan and extent of the early house, but since the remaining tower does not house a main stair, and none such rises in the re-entrant, it is quite likely that the plan would approximate to the letter Z, with this tower at one end of the main block, and another, containing the stair, projecting diagonally opposite.

What remains is a four-storeyed tower with a flat roof, enclosed by an ashlar parapet, borne on a continuous corbel-course, with open rounds at the angles, the roof and the parapet-walk being drained by the usual cannon-like spouts. At second floor level a semi-hexagonal stair-turret of not very graceful design rises within the western re-entrant, to admit to the top storey of the tower, which no doubt served as a watch-chamber. At parapet level the stairway ends in a caphouse with a lean-to roof, from which access is gained to the walk.

Certain windows of the tower have been built up, and that on the first floor has probably been enlarged. A trio of squared recesses have been opened at basement level to hold bee-skeps.

The main block, although containing 16th-century work, is externally so typically of 18th-century construction as to be outwith the scope of a book dealing with the defensive period.

There are two vaulted chambers in the older part of the main block, the smaller opening into the foot of the tower. There is also a vaulted passage. The second storey of the tower is pine-panelled.

The position of the house, on a ridge, protected by a now drained loch on two sides, and a burn and small glen on the other sides, has been a strong one defensively.

Pitcairlie was originally the property of a branch of the Abernethy family. The heiress of Sir Alexander Abernethy married

Sir Andrew Leslie, ancestor of the Earls of Rothes, and brought Pitcairlie into that family. The fourth Earl bestowed it on his second son, Patrick, who became the first Lord Lindores, at the period after the Reformation when the Church lands were being parcelled out. The wealthy Abbey of Lindores, nearby, fell to the Leslies, they having had the foresight to have one of their own family installed as the last Abbot. Patrick Leslie was first Commendator and then temporal lord of Lindores. The second lord, however, despite this sudden accession of wealth, died financially embarrassed at Pitcairlie in 1649, and having borrowed heavily on the estate, it passed to one of the creditors. It was purchased, in the mid-18th century by Colonel James Cathcart of Carbiston, with whose descendants it still remains.

Whether the original 16th-century fortalice was built by the first Lord Lindores or by one of the earlier Leslies is not clear. No doubt the 18th-century extensions were the work of the Cathcart lairds.

PITCULLO CASTLE

The small but most interesting fortalice of Pitcullo is now ruinous, but even so is in a better state than the large modern mansion which replaced it, and which now stands roofless and part-demolished nearby, in hilly country about three miles south-west of Leuchars.

The castle is an L-planned tower of late 16th-century date, the main block of which has been extended in the 17th century by the addition of a square tower. This has been attached to the existing masonry in a most awkward fashion, so that the original south-east angle of the main house projects into the tower to a major degree, allowing only an L-shaped apartment on each floor. The reason for this seems to be partially in order not to interfere with the original windows.

The house, which is three storeys in height, with the stair-wing and addition rising a storey higher, is interesting for two features. The angle-turret which crowns the stair-wing gable is of a most unusual design, consisting of corbelling and pillars enclosing an open space and supporting a stone conical roof. This open work seem to invalidate the turret's usefulness for defence—yet elsewhere on the building are gunloops and shot-holes. There has been another angle-turret on the extension, but of this only the corbelling remains. The second interesting feature is the manner in which the angles of the masonry are chamfered off near basement level. A turret-stair rises in the original re-entrant angle, the main stair in the wing reaching only to first floor level. This stair-turret has been corbelled out to the square at the top, to form a caphouse or watch-chamber, but of this also only the corbelling remains. Another stair-tower rises on the north front, also developed to the square at its summit. A stringcourse enhances the south front of the extension above the first floor. Many of the windows have been built up, and the building is now roofless, save for the stair-wing, and in a state of delapidation.

The entrance is in the foot of the stair-wing and is guarded by a splayed gunloop. The basement is vaulted, and contained two chambers in the main block, that to the west having been the kitchen, with a large fireplace in the gable, with oven and its own window. Behind both the stairs is a small mural chamber at basement level. Owing to the falling away of the ground to the east, an extra semi-subterranean floor has been contrived, un-vaulted, at that end of both main block and extension. From the eastern ground floor vaulted apartment a straight stair leads down to this undercroft, and access is also gained to the northern turnpike stair.

The Hall is the western of the two first floor apartments, and is provided with a mural-closet in the thick western gable, and a fireplace reduced in size. The two upper floors of the stair-wing contain small chambers, which have been panelled.

Pitcullo was a property of the great Fife family of Balfour in the 16th century, and they would be the builders. Previously it had belonged to the Sibbalds.

PITFIRRANE CASTLE

Situated about two miles west of Dunfermline, this ancient seat of the Halkett family is now a clubhouse and its park a golf-course. The first Halkett designated of Pitfirrane is mentioned in a charter dated 1437. He may have built the original fortalice which appears to have been a simple free-standing tower with battlements and caphouse. However, the George Halkett who succeeded to the estate in 1573 made large alterations, and in aspect the older part of the house seems to date from that period. He removed the parapet-walk, raising the walling and adding a squared stair-tower and angle turrets. A carved panel on the stair-tower bears the date 1583 and the arms and initials of George Halkett and his wife Isobel Hepburn of Waughton. Of this George Halkett more hereafter.

The house was again much added to in the late 17th century by Sir Charles Halkett, great-grandson of the above, extending another large L-shaped wing to the east, slightly lower in height. There has been more modern work added to north and east, and a balustraded and enlarged entrance porch inserted in the main re-entrant.

The early work is three storeys and an attic in height, the stair-tower rising a storey higher, with the two upper chambers reached by a narrow turret-stair in the usual manner. The interior has necessarily been much altered to link up with later development, but the usual arrangements would prevail above a vaulted basement.

The 16th-century improver, George Halkett, came to a sad end. He was, in 1585, Provost of Dunfermline, and the General Assembly of the newly Reformed Kirk was to be held in that town, it being 'free of the pest'. Presumably Edinburgh was not. For some reason this did not suit the young King James Sixth, or at least his advisers, and Provost Halkett chose not to offend the civil rather than the spiritual power. He shut the gates of Dunfermline against the fathers and brethren 'alleging he haid the King's expres command sa to do'. The Assembly, with much inconvenience, had to be postponed and eventually was held in Linlithgow. However, the Kirk laughed last, as Sir James Melville in his Autobiography grimly recounts—if without much laughter.

'Bot God within a few yeirs peyit that Lard and Provest his hyre for that piece of service when, for the halding out of his servantes from keiping his Assemblie in that town, he maid his awn hous to spew him out: For ae day in the morning he was fund fallen out of a window . . . wither be melancolious dispear casting him selff, or be the violence of unkynd ghests ludgit within, God knawes; for, being taken upe, his speitche was nocht sa sensible as to declar it, bot within a few hours efter deit.'

This unfortunate's great-grandson, Sir James, was also Provost of Dunfermline. He died in 1705, when the baronetcy which had been conferred on his father, who built the 17th-century extension, expired. The property passed, through the heiress, to the Wedderburns of Gosford, who took the name of Halkett. Sir Peter Halkett was a distinguished officer on the Hanoverian side during the Rising of 1745, and was taken prisoner by Prince Charlie's troops at Prestonpans, and released on parole. When commanded by the Duke of Cumberland to rejoin his regiment nevertheless, he refused, preferring to forfeit his commission. Parliament eventually overturned the Duke's typically unchivalrous action and Sir Peter was restored to his rank, and went as colonel to the American War.

The castle remained in Halkett hands until comparatively recent times.

It is interesting to note that the Halketts for centuries held a charter which gave them the right, presumably exclusive, to export coals. The value of this concession can be gauged by the fact that the Government eventually bought it from them for £40,000.

PITREAVIE CASTLE

This well-known house, celebrated as the source of so many weather forecasts, is now used as a joint Royal Navy and Air Force headquarters, and its policies filled with an assortment of service buildings and hutments. The early 17th century mansion however, with its later extensions, still dominates all, in full use and good order, standing just east of the main road to Rosyth about two miles south of Dunfermline.

It is a tall building of very advanced design for the period, on the double-L or the E-plan, with wings projecting northwards at each end of a long main block, and semi-circular stair-turrets rising in both re-entrants. In the late 19th century extensive alterations were made, a new main entrance and porch fashioned, and the main block extended eastwards. The original house, nevertheless, remains easily distinguishable, and on the north front, practically unaltered externally.

The walling is fine coursed ashlar, not the normal rubble, and rises to four storeys, the gables not being crowstepped as is usual, the windows having broad backset margins. Other unusual features are the peculiar cylindrical bases of the stair-turrets, below the corbelling, fashioned to provide sentry box-like defensive embrasures to guard the doorway, each provided with a narrow slit window with a circular shot-hole in the sill—a device I have not seen elsewhere. The corbelling of the turrets is elaborate, the upper course of which continues along the entire front as a stringcourse. A rectangular garderobe projection is corbelled out on each wing at second floor level—an unexpected feature in a house of this late period. Very noticeable is the symmetrical aspect of the frontage, features on one wing being duplicated on the other, even to the extent of providing an unnecessary doorway, to match the main entrance, which serves only a vaulted cellar unconnected with the rest of the house.

Over the Renaissance main door, which lies in the re-entrant in the west wing, and behind which hangs an iron yett, is a decorative architrave bearing the initials s.h.w. for Sir Henry Wardlaw.

There is an entrance lobby with a sort of guard-alcove with stone seats. It leads to the foot of the former squared main stair, and also to the old kitchens, the westernmost chamber of the main block, the wide fireplace arch of which remains. All the ground floor was originally vaulted, but this was removed in the 19th-century alterations. The first floor contains three large apartments in the main block and one in each wing, the old arrangement of the Hall being here replaced by dining- and drawing-rooms. There is much panelling and good plasterwork ceilings. The two floors above, reached by turnpike stairs in the turrets, provide ample bedroom accommodation.

This handsome house, the arched courtyard gateway for which still survives to the north, was built by Henry Wardlaw, eldest son of Sir Cuthbert Wardlaw of Balmule, Chamberlain to Queen Anne of Denmark, James Sixth's wife. He bought Pitreavie in 1608, and was knighted in 1613. Although there is a handsome sundial in the garden bearing the arms of the third Wardlaw of Pitreavie and his wife, dated 1644, the family did not long retain the property. A picturesque reason for their demise is contained in a tradition that at the Battle of Inverkeithing fought nearby in 1651, when Cromwell defeated the Scots with great slaughter, members of the Clan Maclean suffered greatly. Some came seeking refuge at Pitreavie but the laird drove them off by stones thrown from the roof. The Highlanders cursed the Wardlaws for this, and they lost Pitreavie soon afterwards.

The property later passed to the Blackwood family.

PITTEADIE CASTLE

This most interesting structure, long ruinous but fortunately with its main features still surviving, stands on the edge of a hill two miles north-west of Kinghorn, a pleasant small mansion standing nearby. The building appears to have been originally a free-standing tower of possibly 16th-century date, or earlier, which has been added to and altered in the 17th century. The walls of the original portion are very thick, and it has been entered at first floor level by a removable timber stair, the corbels for the support of which remain—an early arrangement. Corner turrets have crowned all angles save that where the stair-tower rises. This latter is of early 17th-century construction, and finishes in an attractive composition of small watch-chamber with a tiny stair thereto corbelled out in the re-entrant, and containing a miniature fireplace. The basement is vaulted, and so the stone first floor remains, but the others have fallen in. A fine 17th-century Renaissance gateway admits through a high enclosing wall, its tympanum bearing the arms of Calderwood and the date 1686.

Pitteadie was divided Nether and Over, but both portions were united under the lairdship of John Boswell, of the Balmuto family nearby, about 1620. He it would be who made the first 17th-century alterations to an existing tower, probably, by the position, at Over Pitteadie. In 1671 William Calderwood, apothecary and burgess of Edinburgh, purchased the property.

PITTENCREIFF HOUSE

A good example of substantial laird's house at the very end of the fortified period, Pittencreiff stands in what is now a famous Dunfermline public park. Whether built in 1610 or 1651 is not clear, but there is no single defensive feature remaining—vaulting, turrets, slit windows or gunloops. Yet the traditional basic house still shows the old lines—T-planned main block and stair-tower, crowstepped gables and tall sheer walling, with heraldic decoration. Here the top storey is an 18th-century alteration, but the three main storeys are little altered, and the site is a strong one on the edge of a little ravine.

The walls, harled and yellow-washed, rise to three storeys and a garret, the stair-tower being a storey higher to contain the old defensive watch-chamber. This is built out slightly on corbelling, presumably for decoration. The door is still in the foot of the stair-tower, for safety, and is surmounted by a cornice inscribed PRAISED BE GOD FOR AL HIS GIFTIS, and above is a panel bearing the arms of the 17th-century builder Sir Alexander Clerk. Pediments of former dormer windows are built into the walling, one on the west gable also showing the Clerk arms and initials S.A.C.

Although there are claims for the house being built earlier, since the Earl of Dunfermline sold Pittencreiff to Sir Alexander in 1651, that seems a more probable date and in keeping with the architecture.

RANDERSTON

The small but sturdy laird's house of Randerston, now a farm-house, stands in an open windswept position at the tip of the East Neuk of Fife, facing out to sea, about two miles north of Crail. The lands were formerly known as Randolphstoun, from Sir John Fitz-Randolph who swore fealty to the English Edward First in 1296—one of the numerous signatories to the infamous Ragman's Roll, whence came the term rigmarole, meaning nonsense or worthless, as was the value of these Scots' oaths of allegiance. The present building, of course, was not the castle of Fitz-Randolph, which stood on the shore about half-a-mile to the east, but a much more modest building of the late 16th century.

The house is on a variant of the L-plan, three storeys in height, with a circular stair-tower in the re-entrant, which is corbelled out to the square in quite usual fashion to form a gabled watch-chamber above. This tower is provided with protective splayed gunloops at its base. Two angle-turrets project at the north and south corners of the building, but these have been lowered in height, and the modern roof, which is less steep than it would have been originally, now oversails them.

Unusually, the entrance is not in the foot of the stair-tower but at the opposite side of the house, giving access to a corridor serving the two vaulted chambers of the main-block. Also, curiously, the vault in the wing has been reached only through the stair-foot. This appears to have been the kitchen—an inconvenient arrangement for the housewife. The upper floors have been modernised.

By the 15th century the property was in the hands of the lairds of nearby Balcomie, but in 1429 Thomas de Balcomie joined the English army against his King, James First, and his estates were forfeited. For services rendered, the King gave them to Thomas de Myrtoun, Dean of Glasgow. The Myrtons (sometimes called Mortons) remained in possession until about 1629, so a Myrton it was who built the present house. The brother of Moncrieff of Balcaskie bought Randerston, but his line did not last long, for, his grandson being a dissolute character, his father prudently settled the estate on the husbands of his two daughters, one of whom was the Reverend James Sharp, Minister of Crail, and afterwards Archbishop of St. Andrews. The wording of this

legality is much to the point. 'Nov. 1659. The laird of Randerstoun elder surnamed Moncriefe, in Fyfe, departed out of this life
at Randerstoun. He disponed of the tower, fortalice and manor-
place not long before (to defraud his son, a louse liver) to his
two good sonns, viz Kingask, surnamed Ingels, in Cupar, and
Mr. James Sharpe, Minister in Crail.' The writer later mentions
that Randerston was sold to the second son of Balfour of Denmylne. 'It stood him about sextie thowsande merks or thereby.
Ther was as much gotten as payed the old man's debt, the seller's
tochers, and then thowsande merks more, which was to be given
to the young man formerly mentioned (the dissolute son) to help
his portion.'

The estate remained thereafter with the Balfour family.

ROSSEND CASTLE

This fine and historic house, towering on a rocky bluff above the town and harbour of Burntisland, has fallen on evil days; indeed, by the time that this is in print it may well have been entirely demolished, as Burntisland Town Council was so minded at time of writing—a sad fate for an interesting and handsome building that surely should be cherished.

From a small square tower of the early 16th century, later heightened (on left of sketch), a taller wing was extended eastwards later the same century. Early next century another long addition was built westwards, and more modern work later erected against this front.

The original tower rose three storeys to a parapet, the corbels for the support of which still remain. This had open rounds at the angles. The parapet walling has been raised to contain another storey, with modern crenellations. The lower storeys of the tower have been integrated with the later 16th-century addition, and this eastern section contains two vaulted chambers, that to the north being the old kitchen with a wide fireplace in the gable, above which rises the massive chimney-stack seen in sketch.

The entrance was in the foot of the stair-wing, not in the re-entrant as is usual but in the north front. This is still the main doorway, now covered with a modern porch. The Hall is on the first floor, the northernmost of two rooms in the old east block, and has been handsomely panelled in oak. The southern chamber at this level is known as Queen Mary's Room, and has pine panelling of a later date. In this original portion of the tower are large and small mural chambers. Rooms in the 17th-century extension are also pine-panelled.

The main stairway rises only to the second floor, above which the ascent is continued by a small turnpike in the thickness of the walling.

The building is now in a poor state. Most of the windows have been enlarged, and others have been built up. An armorial slab on the north wall above the porch contains the arms of Durie and the date 1554. A former dormer pediment has been inserted high on the north gable, bearing it is thought the arms of Wemyss. Gunloops have lighted the basement vaults of the 17th-century extension.

The name of Rossend is comparatively modern, the castle having previously been known as the fortalice of Burntisland. The lands originally belonged to the Abbey of Dunfermline, but in 1543 Abbot George Durie granted them to his legitimatised son Peter Durie, and they seem formerly to have been occupied by Robert Durie of that Ilk. One of these no doubt built the first tower. Mary Queen of Scots conferred the property on Sir Robert Melville of Murdocairnie, one of her staunchest supporters, and it was while residing here in 1563 that the romantic and tragic incident occurred when the French courtier and poet Chastelard, hopelessly in love with the beautiful young Queen, forced his way into her bedchamber, where he was found hidden, causing Mary in alarm to call for help. At first she ordered her half-brother, the Earl of Moray, to dispatch the offender forthwith with his poniard, but Moray preferred more judicial methods and the unfortunate poet was executed at St. Andrews, crying, 'Adieu, thou most beautiful and most cruel Princess in the world!'

Sir Robert Melville, a loyal adherent of Mary, was forfeited during Morton's grim regency, and the Duries returned. But only for a short time, for Sir Robert got Burntisland back from James Sixth in 1587. It continued with the Melvilles for long, but was garrisoned by the Dundee faction in 1651, and later captured by Cromwell. After 1666 the property was acquired by Sir James Wemyss of Caskieberry, who was created Lord Burntisland for life on marrying the Countess of Wemyss in her own right.

The castle was held by the Jacobite forces of the Earl of Mar for a few weeks in 1715. It was when purchased later in the 18th century by one Murdoch Campbell from Skye that the name was changed to Rossend.

[63]

ROSYTH CASTLE

This is the substantial ruin, with the main features surviving, of an important castle consisting of a late 15th-century tower, almost square but with a slight projection to help house the stairway at one corner, too small to be termed a stair-tower. The site is now in the midst of Rosyth Dockyard, but formerly was a strong one on a foreshore island. The remains of considerable later building surround the keep, and the enclosing curtain wall has been unusually high.

The entrance to the courtyard was by a gateway and pend in the north wall, protected by gunloops and surmounted by weather worn heraldic panels, one of which is dated 1561. The subsidiary courtyard buildings, now very ruinous, dated from this period and the century later.

The keep is built of good quality ashlar, the ten-foot thick walls rising nearly 60 feet to a parapet, unusual in that it merely overhangs the walling slightly and is not carried on the usual corbelling. It is not crenellated, and there are no rounds at the angles. It returns round all the building except the slight projection at the south-east corner aforementioned, which helps to house the stair and which ends in a small gable, forming a sort of elementary caphouse. There has been a gabled garret storey within the parapet, this last having an unusually wide walk of seven feet.

The tower entrance is by a round-headed doorway in the re-entrant, and opens on to a small mural lobby which gives access to a porter's recess, the stair-foot and the vaulted basement. This last has had an entresol timber floor, the corbels for which remain. The first floor contained the Hall, which also had a lofty barrel-vault, with corbels for another entresol or half-floor. The windows are small and have had stone seats. The large window seen in sketch is a 17th-century addition. There are three mural chambers and a fireplace also enlarged in the 17th century. The entresol at this level had its own garderobe with stone seat, in the thickness of the walling. The floor above is not vaulted, but has mural chambers. The garret storey above is now roofless.

The Stewarts of Rosyth were at one time one of the most powerful families in Fife, descending from Walter, High Steward of Scotland. The first of Rosyth Sir David, was a favourite of James First, who erected his Fife lands into the barony of Rosyth in 1428. For 270 years the Stewarts remained in possession, and had many adventures, being forfeited for their activities on occasion. Robert Stewart was a strong supporter of Mary Queen of Scots and he it was who built on the 16th-century gateway to the courtyard, on which he put the initials M.R. for Marie Regina. Curiously enough he was the son of Margaret, daughter of Sir Robert Douglas of Loch Leven, where the unfortunate Queen was imprisoned. His son George died without issue, and the widow, of the powerful house of Murray of Tullibardine, married first the notorious ruffler Archibald Wauchope, Younger of Niddry Marischal, who assisted the Earl of Bothwell and the Master of Gray in their abduction attempt on King James Sixth in 1591. The lady's third husband, Andrew Wood, was no less disreputable, and used to sally out with boon companions to molest and ill-treat seamen at Queensferry and Inverkeithing, in consequence of which he was outlawed eventually. At length, Henry, the late George Stewart's brother, managed to gain possession of the castle. His son, James, who married Margaret Napier, daughter of Napier of Merchiston, inventor of logarithms, opened the large window in the Hall, inscribing it J.S. and M.N. 1639. Because he took the part of Charles First, he was imprisoned in 1647 and fined 3815 merks. The castle was battered, surrendered to and plundered by Cromwell's forces.

There is said to be an inscription on the south side of the building, near the door, as follows:

IN DEV TYM DRAW YES CORD YE BEL TO CLINK
QUHAIS MERY VOCE VARNIS TO MEAT AND DRINK.

SCOTSTARVIT TOWER

Standing on high ground about three miles south of Cupar, Scotstarvit is a handsome and well-preserved fortalice of distinctly antiquated design for the date of its erection. The only date appearing on the building is 1627, and although this is usually accepted as time of building, I suggest that it may only refer to some alteration. A charter indicates that a tower was in existence on the barony of Tarvit in 1579, and might well refer to this building. Even so, Scotstarvit gives a somewhat anachronistic impression, for its style seems to be based on the 15th-century model. Almost certainly it is much later than this, and a charter of 1550 mentions no fortalice on the property.

The tower is L-planned and built of ashlar, not the more usual rubble of this period, the walls rising unbroken five storeys to the parapet. This is borne on individual corbels of an early type, and is provided with circular shot-holes at the angles, with no open rounds. Above is a garret storey within the parapet walk, the steep roof being stone-flagged—another antique feature. The wing contains the turnpike stair, and terminates in a conical-roofed stone caphouse, which gives access to the parapet-walk. Over its door is a heraldic panel with the arms and initials of Sir John Scott and Dame Agnes Drummond his wife, sister of the poet Sir William Drummond of Hawthornden, dated 1627. To 'sky' a panel thus is very unusual, and it may well be a later insertion. There is a peculiar double chinney-stack at the west gable.

The entrance is by an arched doorway in the re-entrant, admitting to a mural lobby, which gives access to the vaulted basement and the stair-foot. The basement retains the corbels to support an entresol or loft floor in the springing of the vault—a common feature of early castles but not in 17th century or later buildings. The windows for this are provided with stone seats. The Hall was on the floor above, its large fireplace subsequently reduced in size. It also has windows with old-fashioned stone seats and a garderobe with sink. There is also a small mural chamber opening off the stair at this level to serve as guardroom. The second floor is a single chamber, also vaulted. The next storey is a poorly-lit room, but having corbels for the support of the flooring of the garret chamber above, which, strangely enough, was a much finer room, well-lit and formerly containing a most ornate heraldic fireplace, now removed to the nearby mansion of Hill of Tarvit. Its lintel again bore the arms and initials of Sir John Scott and wife, dated 1627, and the motto SPE EXPECTO. It is highly unusual to find so much elaboration in a garret chamber, and it is thought that it must have been Sir John's private study, he being a writing man, Director of the Chancery in Charles First's reign, and author of the well-known treatise 'The Staggering State of Scots Statesmen' and other works. It certainly is a room with a view. According to Nisbet, he was 'a bountiful patron of men of learning, who came to him from all quarters, so that his house became a sort of college.' Sir John encouraged Pont to make his famous survey of the whole Kingdom, helping to pay for its publication.

The ground below the tower is also historic. Here lay the army of the Regent Arran, by then created Duke of Chatelherault, which was intended by Queen Mary of Guise to crush the early Reformers. And here was subscribed the treaty which gave the Reformers time, and subsequently led to the establishment of the new religion in Scotland.

The building, though no longer inhabited, is in a good state of preservation.

STRATHENDRY CASTLE

On fairly high ground about a mile-and-a-half west of the burgh of Leslie, stands this excellent late 16th-century tower, now superceded by a modern mansion, but restored, occupied, and in a good state of preservation. Seen from the north (not the view in sketch) it makes an impressive picture, owing to the abrupt falling away of the ground on that side towards a burn-channel, giving a great impression of height. The southern aspect, however, shows details of the building more clearly.

The fortalice is oblong on plan, with a circular stair-tower projecting in the centre of the north front. It is well built of rubble, with the usual dressed stone finishings, and rises to three storeys and an attic. An unusual feature is the small parapet and bartizan that crowns the eastern wallhead only. This is carried on large individual corbels, and there are open rounds at each end—a style reminiscent of at least a century earlier. The attic windows are now semi-dormers, but may have been lowered during some alteration of the roof. Most of the other windows have been enlarged, and others have been built up.

There are two entrances, one in the south front and one in the north, at the foot of the stair-tower. This latter is the more usual place for such, though the rapid falling away of the ground here may have made it inconvenient for the original doorway. The present south doorway does not seem to be original, however, but it may have replaced another close by. There are heraldic panels over both these entrances. That to the south shows a shield halved horizontally (instead of vertically, as is normal) displaying the arms of Forrester above, with Lumsden below, flanked by the initials T.F. and I.L. That to the north is of later work, and consists of a monogram s.e.d., no doubt for Sir E. Douglas, younger son of Douglas of Kirkness, who had married the Forrester heiress and thus acquired the estate. It is dated 1699.

The basement of the tower was originally a single vaulted chamber, but it has been subdivided into three, and the vaulting of the central section removed. In the east gable has been a wide fireplace, so this apartment would be the early kitchen. The first and second floors have two chambers each, modernised but

[68]

retaining moulded stone fireplaces. The top storey has been turned into a single apartment.

In the courtyard is a circular well, and some distance off stands a late 17th-century dovecote.

Strathendry of that Ilk possessed the property from an early date until 1496 when a son of Sir David Forrester of Carden and Skipinch, Keeper of the Rolls, married the Strathendry heiress. The Forrester line, as has been seen, failed again with an heiress two hundred years later, when the Douglas possession began. It passed again through the female line to a nephew, descendant of the old Fife family of Clephane of Carslogie in 1882. Obviously the Forresters built the fortalice as it now stands.

From the doorway of this castle, presumably the northern one, the famous Adam Smith, author of 'The Wealth of Nations' was kidnapped, as a boy, by a party of gypsies (as graphically described in Dugald Stewart's life of Smith).

WEMYSS CASTLE

This most ancient and important castle, occupied by the same family since its erection, stands on a cliff above the shore, between East and West Wemyss. The building, which for a number of years has undergone extensive restoration to its original aspect by its appreciative owner, is a splendid pile, dating from four main periods. The original was an oblong massive tower, of red sandstone ashlar, with a high curtain wall to east and south enclosing a large courtyard, irregularly shaped to follow the line of the rocky site, with a circular drum-tower at the north-east angle. The heraldic decoration seems to indicate a 15th-century date for this, but it may have been earlier.

In the 16th century there were great extensions. The courtyard area was all but filled in with buildings, incorporating the curtain walling, and a round tower thrust out over the cliff to the south —seen on left of sketch, the larger drum-tower on the right, and the main keep not visible. In the 17th century a large L-shaped extension was projected westwards and northwards, doubling the size of the castle. Finally the central space to the north was filled in, in Victorian times, as was the remaining small courtyard. Both of these last have now been cleared away, with excellent effect.

The line of the original curtain walling is still evident, from the fine corbelling for the support of its parapet. Although the upper works have undergone much alteration, the aspect of the castle, from south and south-east, must now resemble the original to some degree. A dormer pediment on the south gable is dated 1671, with the monogram D.L.M.W., for David, 2nd Earl of Wemyss, who built the 17th-century extension, and his heiress Lady Margaret, Countess of Wemyss.

Internally any adequate description is quite beyond the space here available. The basements of the eastern buildings are vaulted, the walling reaching 9 feet in thickness. In the centre of the 17th-century block is a fine panelled oak scale-and-platt staircase. There is much panelling in this part, and a great wealth of excellent pictures.

Sir Michael Wemyss was a supporter of John Baliol, and did homage to Edward of England in 1296. His son, Sir David, was more certain in his loyalties, and was one of the ambassadors sent to bring to Scotland the girl Queen, the Maid of Norway. As Wynton puts it:

'To this passage thae ordanyd then, honorabil knychtis and great men;
Duelland in-to Fyfe war twa, thir the namys war of tha,
Of the Wemys, Schir Dawy, Schyre Mychel Scot of Balwery.'

Generation succeded generation, taking their part in the affairs of Scotland, until Charles First created John Wemyss Earl of Wemyss in 1633. The second Earl, already mentioned built the harbour of Methil at his own cost and was a pioneer of coal development—in which this estate was rich. His heiress daughter married another Wemyss, Lord Burntisland.

David, Lord Elcho, son and heir of the 5th Earl, Prince Charlie's cavalry leader, was attainted for his share in The Forty-five, and could not inherit title or lands. The second son, Francis, adopted his mother's name of Charteris, and was thus enabled to inherit the lands of that family. Eventually David dying without heir, the attainder was reversed in 1826 in favour of the Charteris grandson, who had already succeeded as 4th Earl of March. The present Earl of Wemyss and March is his descendant. However, there had been a third brother in 1746, James, and on him was settled the estates of Wemyss. Since he never changed his name and retained the family property, by law he and his successors became chiefs of the name of Wemyss. Captain Michael Wemyss of Wemyss is the present laird.

KINROSS-SHIRE

ALDIE CASTLE

Situated in a fine hillside position in lonely country about two miles south of Crook of Devon, this is a most attractive example of the traditional Scottish tower-house, sturdy but decorative. After long being ruinous and neglected, it is happily again restored to being a most handsome home.

The building dates from four periods in the 16th and 17th centuries. The original tower of three storeys and an attic has been freestanding. Angle-turrets crown three corners, with a tiny watch-chamber contrived at the stair-head in the fourth or south-west angle. This little room has been reached by trap-door and ladder from the stair-top—instead of the usual corbelled-out secondary stair-turret—which seems a strange economy in a handsome structure otherwise well provided with turrets.

The original doorway lay at this stair's foot. That in the east gable, seen in sketch, is a later insertion. The turrets have each two small windows, giving an all-round field of fire, beneath which are circular gunloops with unusual squared embrasures. Each turret has also a lamp-recess. A massive chimney-stack rises above the north front, with a single dormer window beside it. Another unusual feature is the inverted keyhole-type window at second floor on this front.

The basement is vaulted. The Hall is on the first floor, with an interesting lobby in the thickness of the south wall. The upper floors each contained one large chamber, the joists for the third floor being borne on continuous corbelling.

Although the general aspect of the tower is late 16th century, the mural lobby and the keyhole-type window, both early features, may indicate that a previous fortalice is incorporated.

The first addition was a two-storeyed extension to the south-west, the vaulted basement of which was made the kitchen. Still later was added a larger, three-storeyed range, eastwards, parallel to the main tower, unvaulted. Finally, a century after, the area between this wing and the tower was filled in, and in this insertion the entrance made, guarded by a wide splayed gunloop and another keyhole window. A stringcourse enhances the front of this entrance block. Over the doorway is a worn heraldic panel bearing the arms of Mercer of Aldie. These extensions are all built of rubble, not ashlar as is the main tower.

The castle, tall and now harled and whitewashed, stands out dramatically from the green hillside, seen from the road across the Cleish valley.

The well-known Mercer family, long intimately connected with the city of Perth, are said to have acquired Aldie in the mid-14th century by marriage with Aldia Murray, daughter of Sir William Murray of Tullibardine. In time a Mercer heiress carried it into the family of the Lords Nairne, who in turn passed it in marriage to the Anglo-Irish Lansdowne family, who assumed the name of Mercer-Nairne. From them the present proprietor acquired and lovingly restored the castle.

BURLEIGH CASTLE

This well-known landmark on the eastern outskirts of Milnathort makes an attractive picture. Formerly the seat of the powerful family of Balfour of Burleigh, it was once a much larger establishment than the present remains indicate. The original keep, possibly of 15th-century date, which still stands more or less intact to parapet level, was formerly surrounded by a barmekin or curtain wall, with moat, but of this enclosure only the one wall remains—that connecting the keep to a smaller gatehouse tower to the south. This small tower is still entire, indeed restored, though the keep is ruinous.

The main building, of warm red rubble masonry, is four storeys in height to the parapet, with the remains of an attic storey above. The parapet has been carried on elaborate three-tiered corbelling, and there have been open rounds at all angles save that to the north-east, where the turnpike stairway has ended in the usual caphouse. The entrance, modernised, was in the east front, and gave access to a mural lobby from which the stair-foot was reached. The ground floor is vaulted and would contain the kitchen, with the Hall situated above. There were secondary lean-to buildings within the courtyard.

The smaller tower to the south is interesting and unusual. It is circular at base but is corbelled out to the square to form a watch-chamber on the top floor. This upper storey and roof have been restored. There are wide splayed gunloops at ground level, and small circular shot-holes below the second-floor windows. The date 1582 is inscribed on a skew at the foot of the crow-stepping of the north gable, over a shield bearing the arms of Balfour and the initials I.B. and M.B. This date is typical of the smaller tower's architecture.

The stretch of walling connecting the two towers rises to two storeys and contains a wide entrance archway. There has been a lean-to building on the inner side. Another three-storeyed structure has occupied the south side of the courtyard, but this has not survived.

Burleigh, with its strangely English name, became the property of the Balfours in 1446. Since it was obviously a place of strength, presumably the surrounding level land was marshy, since this site was chosen, to make it inaccessible to attackers. The family was raised to the peerage in 1606, and the fifth baron suffered attainder for his share in the Rising of 1715. In 1707, when Master of Burleigh, learning that the schoolmaster of Inverkeithing had married a young woman for whom he himself had formed an attachment, and on whose account he had been sent abroad to travel and forget, on his return went directly to Inverkeithing and shot the unfortunate dominie, who died twelve days later. The Master was apprehended, tried, and sentenced to be beheaded. He escaped however, and exchanging clothes with his sister, managed to conceal himself successfully for years. His favourite hidingplace was an old hollow ash-tree nearby, which was thereafter known as Burleigh's Hole, which tree was blown down in 1822. He emerged from his secret isolation in 1715, to take part in the Jacobite Rising. Thereafter the title remained in abeyance until the 19th century.

CLEISH CASTLE

This tall and impressive fortalice of the 16th and 17th centuries, stands on rising ground on the northern slope of the Cleish Hills about a mile west of Cleish village and four miles south-west of Kinross. It forms a prominent object from the nearby public road. Although it had become ruinous and abandoned, it was restored around 1840 and has been inhabited since then, so that, like Aldie Castle its near neighbour across the valley, it has happily reversed the depressing fate of so many of these ancient and interesting houses.

The building is on the L-plan, and was formerly within a courtyard, the arched gateway to which is still to be traced in modern outbuildings. The massive walls are unusual in that they are built of good ashlar, not rubble, possibly thanks to the near abundance of an excellent sandstone. They rise to no less than five storeys. It is probable that the present building incorporates an earlier castle, as the angles are rounded on the lower portions of the walling and not above. The house as a whole appears to date from the 16th century, with alterations to the upper works at the beginning of the 17th.

The plan consists of a substantial main block running approximately north and south, of three storeys, an attic and a garret, with a wing projecting to the east, somewhat narrower and seeming to be slightly taller, owing to the falling away of the ground level on that side. An interesting feature is the manner in which the gable of the wing is backset as it rises, giving something of a buttresslike effect. An extra storey is contrived in the wing. On the north front a stair-turret is corbelled out above the lower floors (not seen in sketch). On this turret is inserted the pediment of a former dormer window, bearing the arms of Robert Colville and his wife Beatrix Haldane, and dated 1600.

The entrance was in the re-entrant angle, at ground level, by a moulded doorway, but this is now closed up, the present door being at first floor level, reached by a stone forestair. The early entrance gave access to the main turnpike stair, set within the angle, but internally, not extruded in a stair-tower as is usual. This stair, which rose only as far as the second floor, is now removed. The ascent was continued by the turret stair to the north.

The interior has been much altered in other ways also, and even the vaulting removed from the main block basement chamber. Most of the windows have been enlarged. Nevertheless, Cleish still gives a fine aspect of authentic virility and dignity. It is noteworthy that the flue from the old kitchen fireplace in the vaulted wing basement is no less than 70 feet high.

The Colville family, formerly powerful in Fife and Kinross, owned Cleish for generations. Their arms are amongst those represented amongst ancient Fife families on the famous tempera-painted ceiling at Collairnie Castle in that county. In 1530 Sir James Colville of Ochiltree exchanged those lands for Easter Wemyss and Lochoreshire, Fife, which included the barony of Cleish. Seven years later he bestowed Cleish on his son Robert. It seems probable that the original house was built by this Robert, and the upper works altered by the third Robert in 1600, whose initials have been mentioned.

It was by Cleish that Mary Queen of Scots fled on her escape from Lochleven Castle in 1568.

LOCH LEVEN CASTLE

The famous castle in which the hapless Mary Queen of Scots was imprisoned, stands on an island at the west end of the loch a mile from the town of Kinross. It consists of a 15th-century tower that has stood within a curtain wall dating mainly from later in the same century, with secondary buildings. All is now ruinous, although the original keep remains complete to the wallhead as seen in sketch. The entire enclosure formerly occupied practically the whole area of the island but this has been somewhat enlarged by a lowering of the water.

The courtyard is entered by an arched gateway close to the main keep, and the east and south walls of the enclosure are surmounted by a parapet-walk. There is a circular defensive tower at the south-east angle, with gunloops.

The original keep is oblong on plan and rises five storeys to a flat roof—though this may once have been gabled. The walls, of squared rubble, are approximately eight feet thick. A curious feature is the way that the walling is back-set a little right round at first floor level, only to be corbelled out again at parapet level. The parapet has open rounds at all but the south-east angle in which the stair rises. It is interesting that the lower sections of these rounds are merely solid stonework, with no other purpose than symmetry. Another abnormality is that the topmost storey is lit by windows opening through the parapet itself—something I have not seen elsewhere.

The original doorway is at first floor level in the east front, with a hooded arch, and would be reached by a removable fore-stair. Uncarved shields flank it. From this entrance the Hall is reached, past a screened-off area. It has a fireplace and windows with stone seats. From the screened area a turnpike stair leads down to the vaulted kitchen below. A trap-door in the floor is added for the convenience of hoisting and lowering stores—a sort of service hatch. The kitchen, dimly lit by tiny windows, has a wide fireplace with salt-box, a primitive sink, and a wall-closet with drain. Below the kitchen is another vaulted chamber that could be used as either prison or cellar. It is now reached by the lowermost door, seen in sketch, but formerly was only accessible by trap-door from the kitchen.

The apartment above the Hall has windows in each wall, that

[78]

to the east having been used as an oratory, with altar-shelf and piscina. This may well have been for the use of the imprisoned Queen. There is also a garderobe with seat and drain and another wall-chamber off the south window, having a lamp-recess. The floor above is plainer.

The castle was a royal residence as early as 1257. In that year, Alexander Third and his young queen were forcibly carried off from here to Stirling. It was besieged by the English in 1301, and relieved by Sir John Comyn. Famous prisoners who did not contrive to escape, like Queen Mary, were Archibald Earl of Douglas in 1429 and Patrick Graham, Archbishop of St. Andrews in 1477; both died here. The Earl of Northumberland, who had taken refuge in Scotland after giving offence to Queen Elizabeth, was confined here two years after Queen Mary, before being delivered to his own sovereign for execution. Mary's escape from Loch Leven is too well-known to merit description. At this time the castle had come into the possession of the Douglas Earls of Morton. It seems probable that it was one of these who built the present keep, though no doubt much older work is incorporated.

TULLIEBOLE CASTLE

Tulliebole is one of the most interesting, unspoiled and attractive houses in this volume. It stands in its estate one mile east of Crook of Devon, and not only is in excellent condition but has recently undergone renovation to much of its original authentic state.

Although at first it appears to be a fairly uncomplicated early 17th-century house, of long main block with a stair-wing projecting at one end, investigation proves that there has been considerable early growth and adaptation. Indeed the entire western end may have been a free-standing tower of 16th-century date, and even the eastern section, now dated 1608 and seeming homogeneous, may well have earlier work incorporated.

The building is of three storeys and a garret to the east, and a storey higher to the west. The walls are roughcast and white-washed. The stair-wing is embellished with two angle-turrets of ashlar, and over the doorway, at eaves-level, is a picturesque bartizan, also of ashlar, with machicolations for casting down unpleasantness upon unwelcome guests. The present laird has more kindly utilised this device to provide a high-powered lamp to light visitors in the dark. Such bartizans are seldom seen so late as the 17th century. A tall stair-turret is corbelled-out above first floor in the re-entrant, and there is another circular stair-tower on the north front. A most unusual feature is the curious serpent-like channel and spout to carry rain-water from the bartizan across the front of the easternmost angle-turret.

The door, in the re-entrant, is surmounted by a large and handsome panel, with impaled heraldic devices and initials M.I.H. and H.O., for Master John Halliday and Helen Oliphant his wife. Flanking these are the inscriptions: THE LORD IS ONLIE MY DEFENCE. 2 APRIL 1608, and PEACE BE WITHIN THY WALLES AND PROSPERITIE WITHIN THY HOUS. Interesting is the fact that all the letters N but one are carved wrong way round. Also the day of the month in 1608 is a nicety I have not encountered elsewhere. Four small shot-holes defend the doorway.

The ground floor, strangely is not vaulted—but it is just possible that it may have been originally, for there has been major alteration of floor levels, and the apex of the great arch of the kitchen fireplace shows above the first floor planking. This room, the Hall, reached by a wide squared newel-stair which rises only to the first floor, is a fine chamber which undoubtedly has undergone other alterations than merely changing the floor level, as indicated by a mysterious fireplace, door and window, recently uncovered, high on the east walling—yet not high enough to have allowed for an intermediate floor. Quite the largest Hall fireplace that I have seen graces the west end, with a lintel of one stone slab 11½ feet long, and a salt-box in the south ingoing. The full size of this fireplace, extraordinarily large for the chamber, has only recently been discovered. A private stair in the north walling descends to the basement, no doubt for the laird's convenient access to his wine-cellar, which could be kept locked from domestic interference. To the west is another apartment at this level, and above is domestic accommodation.

John Halliday, advocate, purchased Tulliebole in 1598, and the John who seems to have made the major alterations to an existing fortalice in 1608 was his son, later knighted. Tulliebole was carried to the Moncrieff family by the marriage of the heiress, Katharine Halliday, with Master Archibald Moncrieff, minister of Blackford, in 1705. In due course descendants succeeded to the original Moncrieff baronetcy of Nova Scotia, of 1626, and the eleventh baronet, an eminent lawyer and Lord Justic Clerk, was in 1873 created Baron Moncrieff of Tulliebole. The present laird is 5th Lord Moncrieff, and 15th baronet.

PERTHSHIRE

ABERUCHILL CASTLE

Standing out prominently white against the green wooded slopes of the Glenartney hills, Aberuchill looks very fine across its parkland. It is a large rambling building now, mainly of 19th-century construction, but the original compact fortalice is easy to trace and higher than later work. It stands two miles south-west of Comrie.

The original 17th-century tower has been a typical L-planned structure, with angle-turrets and a circular stair-tower rising in the re-entrant—the opposite side to that shown in sketch. It has one very unusual feature, however, likewise not seen in the drawing. This is the wallhead and roofline at the east end, where main block and wing join. Normally this would finish in the usual crowstepped gable, but here there are twin gables, side by side, each flanked by an angle-turret. The wing itself ends in a gable, so that here we have three gables all bunched together, giving a rather difficult roof system. It would be interesting to know the reason for this device.

The fortalice is three storeys and an attic high, the walls being harled and whitewashed. The dormer windows are modern, but a pediment, presumably from one of the original dormers, built into the west gable, is dated 1607. A modern porch is built out to the south, but otherwise this front is unaltered—as illustrated. The re-entrant on the other side has been completely filled in with 19th-century additions, but the conical roof of the stair-tower can still be seen. The usual arrangement of cellarage on the ground floor, Hall and living accommodation on the first floor, and bedrooms above, would apply. All this has now been altered, of course, to fit in with the modern house.

This was originally MacGregor country, but in due course the

[82]

Campbells won Aberuchill, like so much else, and in 1596 Colin, second son of Campbell of Lawers, was granted a Crown charter to build a fortalice, which is undoubtedly the existing building. Nevertheless, the Campbells did not thereafter have it all their own way, for in the early 18th century the famous Rob Roy MacGregor was making his presence felt to such an extent that the Campbell laird, none other than the Lord Justice Clerk, Lord Aberuchill, actually was a regular customer, or victim, of Rob's, paying his seasonal 'mail' to ensure that his cattle were not taken over by the Gregorach—an extraordinary situation for one of the heads of the Scottish judiciary. After the Rising of 1715, the Justice Clerk's son, Sir James Campbell, seems to have believed that he could now forget about Rob Roy with impunity—the MacGregors had of course been on the losing side, whilst the Campbells had supported the Hanoverian. However, he had the humiliation of having to leave his dinner-table before a houseful of notable guests, and go out purse in hand to buy off the re-doubtable freebooter whose men were all round his castle and his entire herd of cattle neatly rounded up and ready for the road.

ARDBLAIR CASTLE

Whitewashed and surrounded by old trees quite close to the road, a mile west of Blairgowrie, is the delightful and old-world house of Ardblair, making a most attractive picture. Small, compact, and externally at anyrate but little altered since the period of erection, it is fortunate in still retaining its courtyard form so popular with the lairds of the 16th and 17th centuries, but seldom persisting to the present day. Originally it was a strong place, even if such is not now the impression, for the site was once almost surrounded by a loch, now very largely drained.

The earliest part of the building is a tall L-planned fortalice, forming the north and west corner of the courtyard. This has been said to date from 1688, grafted on to the foundations of an earlier tower or keep. This seems too late a date, to the present writer, the general aspect of the work being more typical of the late 16th or very early 17th century. The date mentioned is taken from a heraldic pediment over a fine arched gateway into the courtyard. This however may have been introduced at a later date.

The main house plan is really a variant of the letter L, whereby the wing projects from the main block in such a way as to form a re-entrant angle on both sides—as may be seen from the sketch. This device is useful as a defensive feature, for the commanding of an extra wall-face by shot-hole or gunloop. The slender stair-turret rises in the outer re-entrant. The building is three storeys and a garret in height, though the roof level has been altered somewhat. A handsome and massive chimney-stack rises above the south side of the main block.

The door of the house itself is within the courtyard, in the inner re-entrant and is of remarkably ornate design with an elaborately decorative but empty panel space above. It is guarded by a slit window. The basement is vaulted in the main block, and probably originally contained the kitchen with a wide fireplace below the massive chimney-stack. The wing contains a wide staircase as far as the first floor, above which the ascent is continued by the turret-stair in the usual fashion. The Hall would be on the first floor of the main block, now the dining-room, and panelled in 18th-century style.

The other sides of the courtyard are occupied partly by a retaining wall, but mainly by lower buildings of later dates.

In 1399 Thomas Blair, son of Blair of Balthayock near Perth, received a grant of these lands from David Second. The estate was then a large one, embracing one-fifth of the entire parish of Blairgowrie. The Blairs were notorious as one of the most turbulent families of the land, and normally in a state of feud with the majority of their neighbours. A group of them were summoned for their part in the murder of George Drummond of Ledcrieff and his son in 1554, and for his part in this, Patrick Blair of Ardblair was beheaded. Undoubtedly, in the late 16th century when it would appear that the building took on the shape we see today, Ardblair must have been an exciting place, entirely peaceful as it seems now.

Through marriage the property passed into the hands of the Oliphants of Gask in 1792, which family still own Ardblair today. The Oliphants were notable Jacobites of course, and when Gask was sold about sixty years ago, many relics of Prince Charles Edward and the Rising of 1745 were brought to Ardblair. A sister of the Oliphant who married the Ardblair heiress was Caroline, Lady Nairne, the famous song-writer and poetess. Their father had been Aide-de-Camp to the Prince.

ASHINTULLY CASTLE

Although this must be one of the most isolated occupied fortalices in the county, it was not always so, for in 1677 Andro Spalding its laird got it erected into a free barony, with the right to two yearly fairs and one weekly market. Ashintully Castle itself being declared the burgh of the said barony—an almost unbelievable state of affairs today, when the building stands remotely on high ground within a large hill property about two miles north of Kirkmichael in distant North Perthshire. The country must have been much more populous then, and probably important drove roads converged here.

The building is a comparatively small L-shaped structure of the late 16th century, to one wing of which has been added a considerable extension a century or so later. The keep-like west wing is four storeys and a garret in height, its upper storey and chimneys having been somewhat altered. The most unusual feature of a single open parapet or bartizan that crowns the wall-head above the doorway on the south side, seems to have been renewed as to corbelling and crenellations, but is probably a reconstruction of an earlier defence. The walling is fairly rough rubble, and the windows are very small.

The entrance is in the re-entrant, facing south, and is surmounted by a quite elaborate heraldic panel with the initials A.S. and the date 1583, inscribed THE LORD DEFEND THIS HOUS. There are wide splayed gunloops at basement level facing south, west and east, and at second floor level on the north front a circular shot-hole.

The basement is vaulted, but the kitchen vault has been removed. A straight stair rises in the wing, opposite the door, to the first floor, above which the ascent is continued by a narrow turnpike stair built in a rather unusual position in the thickness of the wall, not in the re-entrant angle but opposite in the outer wall. The normal arrangement of Hall on the first floor and bedrooms above, applied.

Ashintully was for long the seat of the family of Spalding. In 1571 there is a precept from Elchothe (Elcho Castle) by John Wemyss charging Andro Spadyne for the lands of Achyndullie, to meet him, bidden 'in feir of weir' to wait on the King's service at Leith. Andrew Spaldin's wife was a member of the Wemyss

[86]

family, and her initials, now almost indecipherable, A.W., appear at the base of the aforementioned heraldic panel. The Earl of Wemyss claimed the patronage of the parish of Kirkmichael in 1666, which was unsuccessfully disputed by Spalding of Ashintully.

In 1587, a band of 30 men, including Sir James Stewart of Auchmadies, Sir James Stewart of Ballechin, Patrick Butter of Gormack and Patrick Blair of Ardblair, besieged Ashintully and took Andro Spalding prisoner, maltreating him. He seems to have had considerable influence at James Sixth's Court nevertheless, for John Earl of Atholl himself had to become cautioner for his fellow-Stewart culprits, and when they did not appear to stand their trial, after a year's delay, the Earl was actually outlawed, and fined 100 merks for each missing defendant. The fugitives were adjudged rebels, put to the horn, and their goods forfeited. What happened to Spalding is not disclosed.

His successor, David Spalding was himself before the courts four times for supporting the Ruthvens after the Gowrie Conspiracy in 1600. Later, in 1618, he was accused of cutting down and carrying away timber from the Earl of Mar's woods.

Whitefield Castle, nearby, was built on exactly similar plan, but is now very ruinous, unlike Ashintully which is still occupied. It was also a Spalding house.

BALMANNO CASTLE

The tall white, late 16th-century house of Balmanno is a prominent and attractive feature of the northern slopes of the Ochils, near the entrance to Glen Farg.

Built on the L-plan, with a square stair-tower rising in the re-entrant, it has later and lower additions to the north. A slender turret rises from the first floor, containing a smaller stairway and providing room for apartments in the tower above this level, eventually ending in a caphouse which gives access to the open parapet crowning the tower. This is an unusual feature for a fortalice of this period, the open round on the parapet being reminiscent of much earlier work. The caphouse has been heightened and finished with a modern ogival roof. The main block rises to three storeys and an attic, the wing being a storey lower.

Internally, though the house has been modernised, much of the original work remains. The ground floor is vaulted, with the old kitchen now the dining-room. There is a private angled stairway within the thickness of the west wall, that rose to the Hall above.

George Auchinleck purchased the lands from Balmanno of that Ilk about 1570, and built the house soon thereafter. In the mid-18th century the laird was Sir Patrick Hepburn Murray of Blackcastle and Balmanno. It has been handsomely restored by Sir Robert Lorimer in modern times, and is now occupied by a son of Lord Elgin.

BALTHAYOCK CASTLE

This massive square keep occupies a strong position above a steep ravine in hilly ground about three miles east of Perth, with a more modern mansion close by. It appears to date from an early period, possibly 15th century or before, although the caphouse and the parapet around the present flat roof are of late construction. There may well have been a gabled roof within the parapet originally. The floor levels also seem to have undergone some alteration, and certain of the windows have been much enlarged. A heraldic panel with the date 1578 and the initials A.B. and G.M. decorates the walling, but clearly the building as a whole is older than this.

The walls are at least ten feet thick and of very rough masonry. There is a machicolated projection, at second floor level on the south front overhanging the almost precipitous ravine. The present stone forestair up to the main entrance at first floor level is of course an addition; a removable timber stair would be the original defensive feature.

The building, though unoccupied, is in moderately good preservation.

The family of Blair of Balthayock, claiming chiefship of all of that name, was one of the most turbulent and lawless in the land. A chronicle of their offences and feudings would fill this book. Undoubtedly if the stones of Balthayock could speak, they would tell a grim tale.

BALVAIRD CASTLE

Balvaird is one of the most interesting castles in Scotland, and one of the least known. It stands remotely on high ground about four miles south of Abernethy, some way back from a side road. Its position is strong, its appearance spectacular, and it is one of the most advanced examples of castle-building extant.

Although a 15th-century structure, practically unaltered, it demonstrates an improved version of the later popular L-plan and consists of a massive keep, of main block and wing, with a square stair-tower in the re-entrant angle—a feature not appearing generally until over a century later. At this stage it was usual to have the stair within the thickness of the walling, or projecting inwards—reducing the living area. A walled courtyard and gate-house, now ruinous and of probably 16th-century date, extended east and south, entered by an arched gateway protected by a gun-loop, the upper storey of the gatehouse being projected on corbels.

There are three main storeys and an attic, with an extra storey in the wing. A parapet and walk is carried on decorative corbel-ling, with open rounds at all angles, and there is an unusual semi-round in the centre of the north wall, around a chimney-stack. A notable feature is the finish to the stair-tower, which forms a two-storeyed caphouse and watch-chamber combined, itself in the shape of a complete miniature keep, with its own parapet, rounds and crowsteps.

The doorway is in the foot of the stair-tower, surmounted by much worn heraldic panels said to depict the arms of Murray and Barclay. The basement is vaulted, the kitchen occupying the wing. The main block has an entresol, or half-floor within the vaulting, and a pit for prisoners is contrived within the thickness of the walling here. The Hall on the first floor has a fine fireplace with carved lintel and three large stone-seated windows. There is a cosy little wall-chamber alongside the fireplace, and various other mural closets in the thickness of the walls so placed that the flues therefrom run all into one vent, the soil from which fell into a special chamber at ground level, where there was a re-movable stone to facilitate cleaning out—a most exceptional sanitary provision. An ingenious arrangement of stone spouts from the roof enabled these garderobes to be flushed out with rain-water—a forerunner of the water-closet. Removable stones, as above, could be a serious weakness in a fortified house, of course; we know this from the ballad 'Edom o' Gordon' where the besieged lady of the castle condemns a faithless servitor who revealed its position to her attackers, enabling them to smoke her out with a fire against the aperture.

Balvaird was Barclay property, and went with the heiress Margaret on her marriage to Sir Andrew Murray, youngest son of Sir William Murray of Tullibardine towards the end of the 15th century. Since it is the arms of this couple that appear over the doorway, presumably Sir Andrew was the builder. A descendant, the Reverend Andrew Murray, minister of Abdie, was created Lord Balvaird in peculiar circumstances. He was apparently a moderate churchman in days when moderation was not popular. He pleaded for moderation at the General Assembly of 1638—and was in consequence dispossessed of his parish by his angry fellow-clerics. Rather to spite the Kirk than for any other reason, King Charles First thereupon made him Baron Balvaird, he having succeeded to the property on the death of Sir David Murray of Gospetrie, first Viscount Stormont. His eldest son in due course succeeded as second Lord Balvaird and also Viscount Stormont and Lord Scone, all three titles now being held by the Earl of Mansfield, who has on more than one occasion been Lord High Commissioner to the said General Assembly.

The castle, though ruinous, is in a fair state of preservation.

BAMFF HOUSE

Situated in a large estate, amongst the foothill country known as the Forest of Alyth about four miles north-west of Alyth town on the very rim of Perthshire, Bamff is the venerable home of a family which has been established here since as far back as 1232. The house dates from various periods, but the nucleus appears to be a fairly simple free-standing tower probably of the late 16th century, the upper parts of which would seem to have been somewhat modified in the next century. There may well have been still older work to the west, where the remains of a moat are thought to lie.

The tower rises to three storeys and an attic, having crow-stepped gables and dormer windows with decorative finials, but no turrets. The masonry is roughcast, hiding indications of alterations. Wide splayed gunloops of 16th-century type face west at basement level, with an arrow-slit window to the south. Iron bars or yetts have formerly guarded all windows.

The ground floor is vaulted. The Hall on the first floor, like the attractive bedchamber directly above, still retain traces of early panelling.

The Ramsays of Bamff stem from Nessus or Neis de Ramsay, physician to Alexander Second, who had a charter of the lands in 1232. His descendant, Alexander Ramsay, held like appointments to James Sixth and Charles First. Sir Gilbert, his son, was created a baronet of Nova Scotia for his share in the religious wars of the Covenant, in 1666. The present laird, Sir Neis, is 12th baronet.

BELMONT CASTLE

The large modern mansion of Belmont, formerly called Kirklands, all but overwhelms the little fortalice from which it has sprung, in its estate one mile south of Meigle in Strathmore. The site is a flat one, but may well have once been marshy, and therefore strong.

The original building consists of a small and very plain square tower, rising three storeys to the parapet. There is now no garret storey above, but this may have been altered. The present crenellated clock-turret is of course modern, but may well represent the former caphouse at the head of the stairway. The walls, being covered with harling to match the rest of the house, hide clues as to original features, but a single quatrefoil gunloop survives in an unusual position at 2nd floor level. There is a slight batter to the walling at basement level, such as sometimes indicates a formerly soft or marshy site.

The interior has of course been altered to link up with the modern mansion.

Belmont was a property of the family of Nairn of Dunsinane, passing in the 17th century to Sir George Mackenzie of Rosehaugh, the well-known lawyer who earned the name of Bloody Mackenzie for his relentless persecution of the Covenanters. Later the estate came by marriage into the possession of the Wharncliffe family, from whom they were acquired by Sir Henry Campbell Bannerman, one-time Prime Minister. The house is now an Eventide Home.

BLAIR CASTLE

Of all the fortified houses listed in this volume, probably Blair is the most difficult to describe and do justice to. It stands in its own vast estate, about a mile north-west of Blair Atholl, and is of course the traditional seat of the Dukes of Atholl. It is exceedingly large, has grown through numerous phases and extensions, and has undergone three major overall reconstructions in style. Finally, its last reconstruction was a deliberate harking back to an earlier tradition, with a widespread copying of antique styles; so that it is impossible to determine, without minute and laborious inspection, where ancient work ceases and modern begins—the more so as the entire building is harled and whitewashed, thus covering over any clues that different masonry, bond-marks and so on, might offer.

Accordingly it would be pointless to attempt in the space available any detailed description, or indication of the order of erection, especially as each front of the large building shows a very different aspect and contains work of various periods. The sketch of the east front, however, is as revealing as any.

A brief survey of its architectural history may be of value. The first mention that I have discovered is a complaint to the King, in 1269, by David Strathbogie, Earl of Atholl, that John Comyn of Badenoch (grandfather of the Red Comyn slain by Bruce) had begun to build a fortalice at Blair in Atholl. Comyn's, or Cumming's Tower, at the extreme right of sketch, is still so called, but only the foundations can represent this early and no doubt rude stronghold. Thereafter the castle was added to as required by succeeding generations of the powerful Atholl earls of the Strathbogie, Stewart and Murray families. The parapeted and flat-roofed tower, second from right in sketch, gives an impression of early work, by its irregular window-spacing, and this may date substantially from the 15th century. In 1530 the Hall range is said to have been built by the third Stewart Earl. The Stewart line failed in an heiress, who married William Murray, second Earl of Tullibardine early in the 17th century, and as the Tullibardine family was then in high favour with James Sixth, and of great power, no doubt there would be extensive additions thereafter.

However, in 1653, the castle was stormed 'and destroyed

with powder' by Colonel Daniel, one of Cromwell's commanders. Nevertheless, we find it garrisoned by Claverhouse in 1689—here it was that his body was brought for burial after Killiecrankie. Then in 1745 the sad tide of war engulfed Blair again, when it fell to Lord George Murray, Charles Edward's lieutenant-general, to besiege and bombard his own home, occupied by Government troops. It was badly damaged. There followed a still more drastic alteration, for in an access of 'Englishness' the castle was docked of its entire two upper storeys, and all turrets, parapets, etcetera chopped off, the building being remodelled as far as possible as a great plain Georgian mansion, and its name changed to Atholl House. When Queen Victoria visited Blair in 1844 she described it therefore as merely 'a large plain white building.' However, the tide of taste, like war, turned again, and with Victoria's new-found enthusiasm for things Scottish, the then Duke of Atholl had the well-known 'Scottish Baronial' architect, David Bryce, obliterate the outdated Georgian features and restore as many turrets, bartizans and crowsteps as possible.

Any singling out of authentic original detail is therefore impossible; but at least it is safe to say that the present entrance tower, second from left in sketch, is pure Victorian Scottish Baronial, replacing a former Georgian entrance front.

Internally there has been as much alteration. There are a great many very fine apartments, decorated by famous craftsmen, and some vaulting remains.

BRACO CASTLE

Standing deep in a large estate two miles north of the village of
the same name in the parish of Ardoch, Braco Castle is a tall and
very extensive building belonging to four periods, substantial
but plain. The original fortalice has been a square tower or keep,
with a projecting stair-tower, of probably 16th-century construction, though possibly earlier. This now forms the north-west
corner of the building. To it was added, towards the middle of
the 17th century, an extension to the south, engulfing the stair-
tower, and the earlier roof line was altered to link up. This composite group is that illustrated. Then a large L-shaped extension,
of the same height and general style was added to the east,
during the reign of George Third, to form three sides of a
square. Finally the square was filled in with a slightly lower
'castellated' central portion and the sham turrets beloved of the
Victorians.

The earlier parts, with which we are concerned, now make a
fairly homogeneous whole, the lofty rubble walls rising four
storeys and a garret to gabled roofs. The windows have been
largely altered in the 17th century and later, but the small ones
marking the position of the original stair-tower still may be seen.
The small turret perched on the east gable is, of course, a sham.
There are no genuine turrets, gunloops, or any corbelling about
the building. A carved heraldic panel, somewhat weather-worn
but probably depicting the arms of Graham, is set over a ground
floor window in the 17th-century south gable—the only item of
decoration on the entire austere building.

The entrance, which has an unusual semi-octagonal head, lies
at the west and of the oldest portion, indeed at the foot of the
former stair-tower. It gives access to a vaulted passage, and from
this the vaulted ground floor chamber of the early tower opens
on the left, with on the right a non-vaulted 17th-century apartment, no doubt designed as a porter's lodge. Also it leads to the
very good and wide squared stairway of the 17th century, which
has replaced the narrow turnpike in the stair-tower—signs of
which however may still be traced on each floor.

The usual domestic arrangement would apply, of Hall and
living rooms on the first floor and bedroom accommodation
above. There are a number of moulded stone fireplaces. Con-

siderable internal alteration has been inevitable to connect up with later additions.

Braco was a possession of the Graham family, Earls of Montrose. Whether they actually built the original tower is not known, but Braco is quite close to the great Graham lands of Menteith. At anyrate, William, second son of the third Earl—who was a great man, Chancellor and Viceroy of Scotland between 1599 and 1608—was created a baronet of Braco in 1625. This Sir William was therefore the uncle of the famous Marquis of Montrose. He it was, no doubt, who built the 17th-century extension.

The Graham ownership ended with the death of General David Graham at the end of the 18th century.

In 1716 Braco Castle was garrisoned by the Jacobite forces, but abandoned after the disastrous battle at nearby Sheriffmuir. An interesting story relates the building of the large 18th-century extension. The laird of the period, was equerry to George Third. In hopeful anticipation of a visit from his royal master to his home, he added this enormous extension, no doubt partly to accommodate the royal train and partly to enhance his own dignity. Unfortunately the King never came to Braco. It is to be feared that his latter-day successors hardly bless his name today.

BLAIRLOGIE CASTLE

This small fortalice occupies a strong and romantic position on a terrace of the Ochils flanked by a steep burn-channel, overlooking Blairlogie village, three miles from Stirling. The building was originally a free-standing oblong tower, built, it is thought, early in the 16th century, to the east of which a wing was added in 1582, to form an L-plan. There have been later extensions and alterations.

There are two storeys and an attic at the south front but a storey less to the north, owing to the steep rise in ground level. The corbelled-out stair-turret at the south-east angle of the main block seems unusually-placed here instead of within the re-entrant, but of course the wing is of later construction. In this it much resembles Stewarthall in Stirlingshire, just across the Forth. The peculiar oversailing roof and crowstepping seem to argue a lowering of the original roof-level. The two angle-turrets to the west are modern—as is, of course, the large oriel window in the gable. The basement of the original portion is vaulted.

Dormer windows on the early building bear the initials A.S. and E.H., for Alexander Spittal and Elizabeth Hay his wife, dated 1546. Blairlogie came into the possession of the Fife family of Spittal in the late 15th century, and remained so until the marriage of the heiress, Elizabeth Spittal to Robert Dundas of Blair in 1767.

The building is in excellent condition and in appreciative ownership.

CLUNIE CASTLE

One of Scotland's many Clunies, this little fortalice stands romantically on an island in Loch Clunie, between Dunkeld and Blairgowrie. Owing to inaccessability and dense trees, it is to be feared that the sketch is sketchy indeed.

It is built on the L-plan, with circular stair-tower in the re-entrant, unusual in being as wide as the wing itself. The main block is three storeys and a garret in height, the wing rising a storey higher. Obviously the top of the stair-tower, finished off in an extraordinary fashion, possibly not original, contains a little watch-chamber, the twin windows of which may be seen.

The door is in the foot of the stair-tower, protected by arrow-slits. The internal plan is simple, with a room on each floor of main block and wing. The basement contained the kitchen with large fireplace, and the Hall on the first floor was said to have had good pine-panelling at the end of last century.

The fortalice is said to have been built by Bishop Brown of Dunkeld, between 1485 and 1514—though it looks later. His successor, Bishop Crichton, at the Reformation, sold the lands to his kinsman, Lord Advocate Robert Crichton of Elliok in 1562, on condition that they came back to the Church if the Reformation collapsed! This was the father of the more famous Admirable Crichton, who spent much of his boyhood here.

CARDROSS HOUSE

The very interesting old house of Cardross stands in fine parkland on rising ground near the left bank of the River Forth, about two miles south-west of the Lake of Menteith. In former times its site would be a strong one, on one of the few ridges of higher ground in the widespread marshy levels of the Flanders Moss.

The building appears to date from three periods. Originally there seems to have been a comparatively small L-planned free-standing tower-house, with a circular stair-tower in its re-entrant angle, which probably dated from the early 16th century. Then, at the end of that century, to the wing of this fortalice was added, to the east, a long extension of three storeys, the original building being heightened further at the same time. Corner-turrets were added both to the tower and the extension, in the local red ashlar. Later again, in the 18th century, an entirely new north front was added, with still more modern domestic building to the west. The windows were probably enlarged at this period, and the entire roof line renewed, the former crowstepping being replaced by plain gables with ornamental skewputts. Lintels over windows on the south front are inscribed D.E. and M.H. 1598, and I.E. and A.J. 1747. The walls are of rubble, harled and yellow-washed.

An interesting feature is the treatment of the stair-tower in the re-entrant. It is normal for a wider stair to rise only as far as the first floor, where are situated the public rooms and Hall, above which a narrower stair is corbelled out in a long turret to give access to the private accommodation. In the case of Cardross, this arrangement is achieved by using the one circular stair-tower, making it wide as far as the first floor, and thereafter narrowing it in abruptly and considerably, to rise right up above roof-level, where it ends in the usual conical roof. Whether this is original or part of the late-16th-century alterations, is uncertain.

The early entrance, now closed up, was in the foot of this stair-tower, the normal position. Curiously enough the basement of the main block of the original fortalice is not vaulted, unlike that of its wing, which was the early kitchen. It is possible that this vaulting has been removed. The ground floor of the later 16th-century extension consists of a series of vaulted cellars reached from a long corridor from the earlier wing. The Hall, on the first floor of the early tower, is a delightful chamber, though modest in size, still panelled in Memel pine. Excellent plaster ceilings enhance the first floor apartments of the extension, one said to be of 16th-century date, the other, more classical in style, belonging to two centuries later.

Cardross was long a seat of a branch of the Erskine family, stemming from the Earls of Mar. John 2nd Erskine Earl, received from his schoolmate and early companion, James Sixth, the Abbeys of Cambuskenneth and Dryburgh, and the Priory of Inchmahome. David Erskine who died at Cardross in 1611 was Commendator of Inchmahome, which of course is nearby, on an island in Lake of Menteith, and Henry Erskine of Cardross was the last nominal and secular Prior thereof. There is a tradition that Cardross was garrisoned by Cromwell's troops for ten years —which seems excessive. Its proximity to Flanders Moss and the stamping ground of Rob Roy MacGregor, must have ensured it of considerable activity for many a day. The house, fortunately, is in excellent order, and lovingly cared for by its present owners, Sir Ronald and Lady Orr-Ewing.

DRUMMOND CASTLE

This famous stronghold of a famous family stands in a dominating position on the highest point of a rocky eminence in its large estate, three miles south of Crieff. The present buildings date from three distinct periods; a tall 15th-century square keep, a lower early 17th-century extension of it, and divided from these by a wide courtyard, a large and comparatively plain mansion of later date.

The soaring keep, built on the highest point of the rock, was erected soon after 1487 when Sir John Drummond first purchased the property, moving here from Stobhall near Scone. It is five storeys and a garret in height, with very thick walls, and is crowned by a renewed parapet with open rounds at the angles. A square stair-tower projects on the east side, and another, part-buttress, part-tower, rises at the north-west angle, as seen in sketch, similar to that at Kinnaird Castle in the Carse of Gowrie. The building was very badly damaged by Cromwell, and again was partly demolished by its countess after having been garrisoned by Hanoverian troops after the Rising of 1715, so that such occupation should not be possible again; however, the restoration of 1822 has been discreet and in keeping with the original style. Iron yetts or grilles still fill many of the windows.

The entrance is at first floor level on the inner or courtyard side, and no doubt was originally reached by a removable timber stair, for security. Now a stone forestair rises and gives access to the Common Hall on this level, protected by a guardroom, from whence a narrow stair within the thickness of the walling descends to the vaulted basement, which would serve as a prison. A turnpike stair in the tower projection leads up to the principal Hall above, a fine apartment, well lighted, its windows having stone seats. The upper floors have been modernised.

The entire keep is now preserved as a museum and armoury.

The early 17th-century extension is attached to the south, and forms a three-storeyed gatehouse block. It is a simple oblong gabled building with dormer windows, through which an arched gateway pend is slapped, still provided with its massive double wrought-iron gates. Above is a heraldic panel. To the right of the pend is the vaulted porter's room, or guardroom, recently restored. Above was additional domestic accommodation for the keep. The dormers bear the Drummond arms, with the initials of the first Earl of Perth and the dates 1630 and 1636.

Another range of building, dating apparently from the same period, has occupied the very rocky site to the north, but of this only foundation traces remain.

The builder was twelfth in descent from the founder of the family, a Hungarian called Maurice who arrived with St. Margaret the Queen at the Court of Malcolm Canmore, and took his name from the lands of Drymen or Drummond which he was granted in West Stirlingshire. His successors greatly distinguished themselves, notably Sir Malcolm at Bannockburn, and were rewarded with large lands in Perthshire. The daughter of the builder of this keep was the fair Margaret Drummond, beloved of James Fourth. He desired to marry her, but was under enormous pressure to wed Margaret Tudor, Henry the Eighth's sister, for the sake of the realm. Margaret Drummond with her two sisters, was poisoned here at Drummond Castle in 1502, presumably to ensure that the King made the right diplomatic choice, to his undying grief. James was a frequent visitor here, naturally, as was his granddaughter Mary Queen of Scots.

The fourth Earl followed James Seventh and Second into exile, and by him was created Duke of Perth. For supporting the Stuart cause in 1715 and 1745 the family was banished and their estates forfeited, eventually passing through the female line to the English Lord Willoughby de Eresby and thence to the Earl of Ancaster, the present owner. The estates were unsuccessfully claimed by the male line descendant, the Earl of Perth, in 1868.

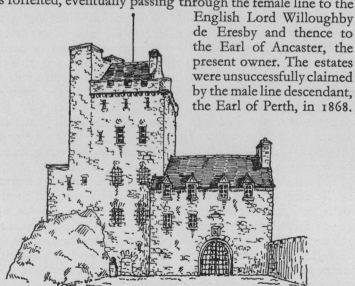

EDINAMPLE CASTLE

Here is another of those properties which the acquisitive Campbells must have managed to wrest from the MacGregors when that proscribed and ill-fated clan were in low water—and only a few miles east of the Gregorach last-ditch rallying ground of Balquhidder. That there was a fortalice on the spot before the Campbell times seems to be indicated, for though the ancient part of the present castle appears to be a typical example of the late 16th-century Z-plan, internal evidence suggests that there is a smaller and earlier tower incorporated in the eastern portion of the building.

Today, Edinample is a tall, whitewashed and attractive structure, set picturesquely on a steeply sloping hillside on the south side of Loch Earn, near its head, where the double waterfalls of the Ample Water tumble down from the high hanging valley under Ben Vorlich. Closer inspection reveals that a high four-storeyed addition has been attached to the south, and a two-storeyed combined porch and stairway erected against the north front, somewhat detracting from the appearance.

The early fortalice consists of a substantial main block of four storeys and a garret, with large circular towers projecting at the north-west and south-east corners. Unfortunately the high later addition to the south has completely enclosed the south-east tower—but it is still there, within the building, with its moulded stone main doorway and coat-of-arms above. It is at this corner that the original pre-Campbell tower seems to have stood. Two three-storeyed stair-turrets, corbelled out above first floor level, give access to the upper floors in angles between round towers and main block.

The ground floor contains three vaulted cellars, with another in the foot of the north-west tower. The south-east tower contains the main stair, rising only to the first floor. Two of the main block cellars have private stairs rising within the thickness of the walling to the first floor, one to the Hall and one to the east of it, ending in the ingoing of a window. Lairds quite normally liked to have a private stair down to their wine-cellars, the doors of which they could keep locked; but two such is unusual, and probably that to the east is a relic of the earlier fortalice.

A grim and unpleasant bottle-dungeon is contrived in the

thickness of the south-east tower walling. The only access to this
is by a narrow trap-door in the floor of the little guardroom
above—so narrow that the shoulders have to be inserted this way
and that in order to get through the gap. Thereafter a ladder
leads through the neck of the 'bottle' down into the complete
darkness of the dungeon proper, which appears to be about
sixteen feet deep and five feet in diameter. One wonders how
many unfortunate MacGregors have lodged here? The guardroom above is provided with a narrow gun-slit facing east.

At this level, in what is now an internal lobby of the more
modern extension, may be seen the heraldic panel already mentioned. It depicts the Campbell arms, quartered with what looks
like a Stewart coat, under a knight's helmet and the initials c.c.
There is no date, but the general aspect of the work suggests a
late 16th-century construction, and the builder was no doubt
one of the many Sir Colin Campbells.

ELCHO CASTLE

This famous castle represents a high standard in the development of the fortified tower-house into comfortable mansion. It stands on a slight eminence on the low south bank of Tay four miles east of Perth—not at first glance a strong position, but not only cliffs and ravines provided defensive features; marshlands and river-banks, as here, could be equally effective, aided by a system of outworks and ditches. Elcho was indeed early known as a strong place, and provided sure sanctuary for Wallace frequently.

Space forbids any comprehensive description of the complicated and elaborate structure. Basically however it consists of a large oblong main bloc, with a square parapeted tower rising at the south-west angle, and three more towers projecting on the north side, two of them round stair-towers corbelled out to the square at the top to form watch-chambers, the third merely containing a small apartment on each floor. There is a large angle-turret at the south-east corner, and numerous corbelled projections elsewhere.

Save for the square south-west tower, which is fairly typical 15th-century work, with its normal parapet and open rounds, the upper storeys of Elcho do not really match its massive walls, innumerable old-style gunloops and the many mural chambers of the lower storeys. Probably there was a drastic reconstruction of the main block in the second half of the 16th century, when these upper works would be added. Certainly none of the present work dates from the period of Wallace, so that there was no doubt an earlier castle on the same site.

There is much accommodation on all floors. A fine roomy turnpike stair in the foot of the south-west tower has steps seven feet wide. The handsome vaulted kitchen on the ground floor has an enormous fireplace as large as a room, and its great chimney-stack enhances the north front. The large Hall on the first floor has no fewer than three stairways up to private rooms. The provision of so many gunloops all round the walling is striking, as are the fine iron yetts still guarding so many windows. The entrance, in the foot of the square tower, is defended by an unusual type of machicolated projection up at parapet-level.

The lands of Elcho have been possessed by the Wemyss family for nearly 500 years, their first recorded charter, dated 1468, being a grant from James Third to John de Wemyss, son and heir of Sir John Wemyss of that Ilk. Another Sir John, in 1633 was created first Earl of Wemyss at the Coronation of Charles First at Holyroodhouse—though in the Civil War that followed, the Earl took the side of Parliament against the King. On the remains of a round tower seventy yards to the south-west, part of outer defences, are the initials E.J.W. thought to refer to this John, Earl of Wemyss—though these fortifications are of a much earlier date than 1633.

David Lord Elcho, eldest son of the fifth Earl, took a prominent part in the 1745 Rising, was present at Culloden, but escaped to France. He was declared a rebel, but his father having taken no part, the estates were not forfeited, so that the earldom passed to his younger brother who had adopted the surname of Charteris. Shortly after this, Elcho Castle seems to have been abandoned as the family residence.

History was not quite finished with Elcho yet, however, for in the great grain famine of 1773, a mob marched from Perth to the castle, which was being used by a local farmer as a storehouse for grain to be exported to England and France where higher prices ruled, and only soldiers prevented a riot and the burning of the castle. The grain was sold in the open market in Perth next day.

Elcho is now in the care of the Ministry of Works.

EVELICK CASTLE

Situated high amongst the Sidlaw foothills in Kilspindie parish about 5 miles from Perth, this substantial ruined stronghold is interesting, notably because of the great number of gunloops provided, there being one for almost every window-breast.

The building appears to date from the early 16th century, and is built on a variation of the L-plan, with two wings joining at their corners, and a semi-circular stair-tower rising in the south-west re-entrant. The walls rise three storeys to the wallhead, but the attic storey above has disappeared, save for the gunloops for its dormer windows. Certain of the windows have been enlarged. The fabric is not in a good condition, and is much broken down to west and south. There have been extensive outbuildings.

There appear to have been two doorways, but possibly that in the northern re-entrant is a later provision, although protected by gunloops. The main entrance is in the foot of the stair-tower, and above is an empty panel-space. The basement has been vaulted, but this, with the floors above, has fallen in.

The Lindsays of Evelick descended from Earl Beardie of the Crawfords. Andrew Lindsay was created a baronet in 1666, and his second son Thomas was the victim of a particularly brutal murder here at the hands of his step-brother James Douglas. During a game, Douglas stabbed Lindsay five times, then held the dying youth under water in a burn, and finally dashed his brains out with a rock.

The last of the Lindsays was drowned in 1799.

INVERMAY TOWER

Standing near the later large mansion in a picturesque estate where the minor River May debouches into the Earn, three miles from Dunning, this small but sturdy fortalice is an L-planned structure of probably late 16th-century date, added to later. A main block of three storeys has a stair-tower projecting at one end. Another lesser semi-circular tower has been added in the centre of the opposite front, the door of this being dated 1633.

The stair-tower is corbelled out above second floor level to contain a small gabled watch-chamber, reached by a tiny turnpike stair, the semi-circular projection for which can be seen in sketch as an embryo turret. A keyhole-type arrow-slit guards the door in the foot of this tower. The main block has been extended on this side in rather clumsy fashion; thus the two-storey range seen left of the tower is of later date.

The building is not now occupied, but is maintained in a fair state.

The Belshes family of Invermay stemmed from the Norman, Ralf Belasyse. The first of Invermay was Alexander, son of John Belshes of Tofts, Berwickshire, married to the daughter of Sir Thomas Murray of Glendoick, Lord Clerk Register, in the late 16th century, and heiress of Patrick Hepburn of Blackcastle, a Protestant cleric turned Catholic again, who married Mary Queen of Scots in a private Papistical ceremony after her public Protestant wedding to Bothwell.

FINGASK CASTLE

Standing in a wooded glen above the Carse of Gowrie, about four miles north of Errol, Fingask is a very delightful and attractively situated house which has suffered many vicissitudes, historically and architecturally. Today, happily, it is restored to approximately what it was in its best and authentic period, with a great deal of later and pretentious additional work cleared away. Unfortunately in the process it has lost its square stair-tower from the re-entrant angle; but otherwise the early southern range is more or less as it was when built.

The original building is on a modification of the favoured L-plan, with a slight extension of the main block westwards. The substantial mason-work is of good coursed rubble of a warm red-brown shade, the walls rising to three storeys and a garret. There are now no towers or turrets remaining, but a number of the original gunloops and shot-holes survive, as do the iron yetts over certain of the windows. Built into the walling are the heraldic pediments of former dormer windows, displaying the arms of Threipland.

The present doorway, near the re-entrant angle, if not actually the original one, is very close to where it must have lain in the foot of the stair-tower that formerly rose here. The curved inner face of a section of this tower can still be discerned externally, in the angle. The door is well-protected, the vaulted guardroom adjoining in the passage to the right having no fewer than four gunloops facing in various directions. In the foot of the wing, at basement level, is the vaulted kitchen, with an enormous arched fireplace in the gable—in the back of which are two small windows and another gunloop. Still another gunloop faces north. The impression gained from all these defensive features is that the builders had little sense of abiding security—as indeed their history proves.

The Hall on the first floor is a handsome apartment, with a smaller room in the wing opening off it, both well provided with garderobes and wall-closets. Above is the usual domestic accommodation.

The building as described dates substantially from 1594, although there is probably a still older nucleus incorporated, to account for the mural chambers and the thickness of the walling.

There were additions in 1675 to the west, lower in height, and a long modern wing stretches to the north, all the remaining work being now, fortunately, architecturally harmonious.

The earliest owners were a branch of the great Bruce family of Clackmannan. They sold Fingask to the Threiplands, who had migrated north from Threipland in Peebles-shire. Patrick Threipland, Provost of Perth, was knighted in 1674 for diligence in suppressing conventicles, created a baronet in 1687, and died a prisoner in Stirling Castle two years later. His son, Sir David, was one of the first to join the Earl of Mar's standard in the Rising of 1715, and his eldest son was captured in the daring crossing of the Forth in Mackintosh of Borlum's famous raid on Edinburgh—making a dramatic escape from Edinburgh Castle later. The Old Chevalier twice stayed at Fingask in 1716. After the Rising had been defeated, the estate was forfeited and occupied by dragoons. This happened again in the next Jacobite Rising of 1745, when the elder son fell at the Battle of Prestonpans. His brother, Sir Stewart however, went through the entire campaign with Prince Charles Edward, sharing many of the Prince's subsequent wanderings, obtaining a small part of the almost legendary Loch Arkaig Treasure, and finally escaping to France disguised as a bookseller's assistant. He returned to Edinburgh in 1747 and set up as a physician, and was later able to buy back his forfeited inheritance of Fingask. The baronetcy, also forfeited, was restored to his son Patrick in 1826.

Although there are no Threiplands at Fingask today, their memories permeate this most mellow and attractive house that looks out from its pleasant gardens over such a fine panorama of the Carse and the Tay to Fife.

FOWLIS CASTLE

Now a farmhouse, this tall fortalice stands on high ground about six miles north-west of Dundee, a prominent landmark. Both parish and castle are properly known as Fowlis Easter, to avoid confusion with Fowlis Wester near Crieff, and Foulis Castle in Ross.

The present building is the latest part of what was once a great and powerful stronghold, with a large quadrangle, high outer walls, corner towers and portcullis, one of the main seats of the influential and warlike Lords Gray. What remains was known as the Lady's Tower, or Bower, and dates apparently from only the early 17th century, although almost certainly earlier work is incorporated in its lower masonry, since the wide splayed gunloop at the foot of the massive lofty chimney-stack seems to belong to an earlier period.

The remaining structure is a very simple oblong building, to which a more modern wing has been added to the north, with a circular stair-tower and the notable projecting chimney-stack rising on the south front, as seen in sketch. This chimney, which houses the flue for the huge kitchen fireplace, is the house's most outstanding feature, and is offset at each floor level as it rises. The building contains three storeys and an attic, the stair-tower rising a storey higher. The dormer windows, at roof-level, unfortunately are now built of unsightly naked brick, but the triangular pediment of one of the originals is built into adjoining property, and contains the date 1640. The conical roof of the stair-tower is modern also, for some time ago this was slated over flush with the main roof, as previous drawings show. Nevertheless, the original would certainly have a conical roof of this sort, though probably not quite so high-set.

The main doorway lies in the foot of the stair-tower, as is usual, but this did not connect with the kitchen which occupied the whole of the ground floor space (though this is now subdivided). This door gave access at once to the turnpike stairway and the upper floors. A back door for the kitchen is now opened in the east gable, but this may not be original. The building was never, of course, intended to be free-standing and self-contained, being only part of a much larger establishment. The structure is now in good condition and occupied, though at one time, after having served as a village alehouse, it fell into a very bad state of repair.

Fowlis Easter was granted by King David First to William de Maule, for gallantry at the Battle of Sauchie in 1138, passing to the latter's son-in-law William de Mortimer. It remained with the Mortimers until it went by marriage in 1377 to Sir Andrew Gray of Broxmouth, the first Gray to move up from the Borderland to these parts, which they were later to dominate, and who became the first Lord Gray of Fowlis. That great and often superlatively wicked family, who also built Castle Huntly not far away, and owned Broughty Castle likewise, as well as many lesser strengths, retained possession until 1669, when the ninth Lord sold it to the Murrays of Ochtertyre. It is perhaps a sobering thought that some of the worst treacheries and Machiavellian misdeeds to stain even Scotland's history were concocted under the roofs of either Fowlis or Castle Huntly—including the betrayal of Mary Queen of Scots and secret intrigues with Queen Elizabeth to encompass the hapless Mary's death, by the Master of Gray. If these stones could indeed speak . . .

GARTH CASTLE

Despite its stark plainness, Garth Castle is one of the most interesting fortalices in this county. It stands in an immensely strong position above the precipitous confluence of two burns, perched like an eagle's nest on a crag on the steep west side of the Strath of Appin about a mile north of Coshieville. Although long a ruin it is now happily being restored for occupation.

The building is grimly functional, without any sort of decoration, architectural or heraldic, and is clearly of great age. Its erection is ascribed to Alexander Stewart, the celebrated or notorious Wolf of Badenoch, fourth son of Robert Second and grandson of The Bruce, who died here in 1396. There seems to be no reason to doubt this antiquity.

The tower is practically square on plan, with walls of unhewn boulders, 6½ feet in thickness, rising 60 feet to the parapet. Not even the quoins or cornering stones are of ashlar. There is no corbelling of any sort, and the parapet rises flush with the walling. There has been a gabled garret storey above that level, but it appears that the parapet has crowned only the east and west wallheads.

The entrance is at ground level to the south, the only access thereto being a steeply climbing footpath. A strong iron yett still guards this doorway. The stairway commences within the thickness of the walling immediately to the left, a notably narrow straight stair, only 2 feet in width, which continues to rise round all four sides of the building, to the parapet. The basement consists of two vaulted pits, lit only by arrow-slits. The first floor, also vaulted formerly, was the Hall, with a huge fireplace and windows with stone seats. Another vaulted storey above contained bedchambers, with the upper floors providing dormitory accommodation for men-at-arms.

There are many tales of the Wolf of Badenoch's lawless activities from this stronghold, which must have seen stirring times indeed. These did not cease by any means with its builder's death, for his successors seem to have been of the same kidney. In 1502, for instance, Nigel Stewart of Garth led a raid on nearby Weem Castle, burned it, and took Sir Robert Menzies prisoner, putting him in the vaulted dungeon at Garth and threatening to starve him to death unless he signed away sundry rights to the Stewarts.

James Fourth was very angry, and commanded that castle and captive be surrendered immediately—and when this was refused, proceeded in person to take action against his distant cousin. The Earl of Atholl, Garth's father-in-law, managed to save Nigel from the gallows. At a later date he is suspected of arranging the murder of his own wife, by having one of his followers kill her in the burn below the castle 'negligently, by the blow of a stone'. Thereafter he was kept imprisoned in his own tower for nine years, it is said, until his death in 1554. He was the last of the actual Barons of Garth. Thereafter the property passed to a neighbouring branch of the Stewart clan, of Drumcharry, also descended from the Wolf of Badenoch through the Bonskeid Stewarts.

The castle remained inhabited until the middle of the 18th century, when William Stewart built the house of Drumcharry, on the site of the present Garth House, nearer Fortingall. Of this line came the noted soldier, administrator and author General David Stewart of Garth. The estate was bought by Sir Donald Currie in 1880, who partially restored the castle. It will be most interesting to see this venerable pile once again occupied.

GLENDEVON CASTLE

Situated on high ground in the centre of Glendevon, at the southern extremity of the county, this much altered fortalice stands about four miles north of Yetts of Muckhart on the Gleneagles road, and is now a farmhouse. The building, which appears to date mainly from the early 17th century, displays a number of unusual features. It is on the Z-plan, and has once been a commodious dwelling and strongly sited, consisting of a main block with a square tower projecting at the north end and another in the opposite direction at the south. Only this south tower remains complete, the building having suffered a drastic lowering in height, and the roof-line finished in an extraordinary mixture of lean-to slating and sham crenellations.

The south tower is four storeys in height, ending in a gabled roof without crowstepping. Unseen in the sketch, a circular stair-tower projects to the west at the junction of the south tower and the main block, finishing in a conical roof. The walls of both south and north projecting towers are considerably less thick than those of the main block—the east wall of which measures no less than 9 feet—indication that this contains the remains of a much earlier castle. It would appear therefore that the original structure was a simple massive oblong tower or keep, possibly of the 15th century, probably with this semi-circular stair-tower projecting at its south-west angle, to which the square towers were added later.

There are two doorways. The main entrance lies in the foot of the tall south tower, admitting to the squared stairway. Over this doorway there was, in living memory, a panel bearing the motto PER MARE PER TARRIS, the initial R and dated 1766. Presumably this commemorated the passing of the property to the Rutherford family. The panel-space is now empty. To the right of the stair-way a passage leads to the vaulted basement of the tower, which is windowless.

In the south wall of the main block is another doorway protected by a gunloop. The basement of the main block contains two vaulted apartments having no communication with the upper floors. That to the right may have been the kitchen, although if so, it was very ill-lit, with a fireplace in the thick east wall and adjoining it a large mural chamber or recess, provided with a shot-hole. The other cellar is entirely plain. These vaults are now used for farm storage.

The Hall, now the farm living-room, is on the first floor of the main block. Above this level there are now chambers only in the south-west tower, these being reached by a turnpike stair within the circular stair-tower.

Glendevon Castle is said to have belonged to William, Earl of Douglas, who was treacherously tricked, accused and arrested at a royal banquet, known as The Black Dinner, by Livingstone and Crichton, then largely ruling Scotland in the names of James Second; he was thereafter executed as a traitor, along with his brother and another relative. This deed was to cost the young king dear with the great clan of Douglas—although some accounts declare that James tried hard to save Douglas from the violence of his favourites. This was in 1452.

> 'Edinburgh Castle, toune and towre,
> God grant thou sink for sin!
> And that even for the black dinoir
> Earl Douglas gat therein.'

The massive east walling of the main block quite possibly dates from this period. Otherwise history is very silent about Glendevon. It is recorded that it was restored from a ruinous condition in the 16th century by one of the Crawford family, but clearly there have been later alterations than that.

GRANTULLY CASTLE

This quite spectacular and unusual house stands in pleasant country on the south bank of the Tay less than 3 miles from Aberfeldy. Although it contains older work, it dates essentially from the late 16th century, with notable alterations made less than fifty years later. A large modern mansion, in the same style of architecture, has been added to the north and east.

The fortalice as it stands, three storeys and a garret in height, of warm-coloured local rubble, conforms to the Z-plan, of oblong main block with square towers projecting at opposite angles; it also has the unusual addition of a tall circular stair-tower rising in the south-west re-entrant. From the great thickness of the main block walling, however, it appears that it incorporates a free-standing square keep of earlier date. The heightening of the circular stair-tower to form a watch-chamber, with its late ogee roof, the dormer windows, and probably the angle-turrets, date from 1626, when it seems that the entire upper works and roof-line were remodelled. The walls are provided with gunloops, one sited in a rather peculiar position half-way up the south-west tower.

The entrance is in the foot of this south-west tower. Normally it would be expected that the stair would rise in this tower, but the provision of the circular stair-tower behind permits instead a guardoom at ground floor level, to protect the doorway and secure an unpleasant underground pit of prison directly below, only reachable from the guardroom floor—an arrangement typical of an age earlier than the 16th century.

The ground floor of the castle is vaulted, that of the main block consisting of two parallel cellars. In the north-east tower basement is the old kitchen, but this again seems to be a re-arrangement for there was no original internal entrance thereto. The Hall was a square chamber on the first floor, wood-panelled. A passage formed within the thickness of the east walling at this level led to what would be the laird's private chamber in the north-east tower—another antique provision. There are garderobes opening off this passage.

A peculiarly placed dormer window on the circular stair-tower is dated 1626, and displays the arms of Stewart. Grantully came into the possession of a branch of the great house of Stewart as early as the late 14th century, in the person of Sir John Stewart, second Lord of Innermeath and Lorn, fourth in descent from Alexander 4th High Steward of Scotland. The original castle, said to have been built about 1414, is supposed to have been sited about one mile to the east—which raises a problem with regard to the ancient work incorporated in the present fortalice; It seems unlikely that there should have been two strong 15th century castles at Grantully. Be that as it may, most of the remaining house dates from the late 16th century, with the upper works much altered by Sir William Stewart, Sheriff of Perth, and his wife Agnes Moncrieff, in 1626. The baronetcy acquired by this family expired towards the close of last century, by which time the building was deserted and semi-ruinous, the family having moved to Murthly Castle in the same county considerably earlier. It is interesting to note that Grantully is not only handsomely restored, but in occupation once again by members of the same family as that of Murthly.

Occupying an important strategic position, the castle was successively used as headquarters by various military commanders, including Montrose, General Mackay, Argyll, Mar of the Fifteen Rising, and Prince Charles Edward. It is told of General Mackay's occupation, that after the defeat of his Government troops at Killiecrankie, one of his soldiers had a dispute with an officer, and shot him dead in one of the angle-turrets here, the blood staining the floor and said to be permanently visible.

HUNTINGTOWER

This well-known and impressive fortalice, originally known as Ruthven Castle is immortalised in the song:

'Blair in Atholl's mine, Jeannie, Little Dunkeld is mine, Jeannie,
Saint Johnstone's Bower and Huntingtower, and all that's mine is thine
Jeannie.'

The singer was one of the Murrays of Tullibardine and Atholl, who gained this property and changed its name to Huntingtower after the fall of the Ruthven family who built it.

Standing about three miles from Perth, near the south bank of the Almond, the castle though it now looks all of a piece, represents in fact three distinct periods of building. The original structure was a simple free-standing tower of three storeys and a garret, oblong on plan with the usual parapet and open rounds at the angles. This is the building on the right of the sketch, and probably dates from the early 15th century. Towards the end of the same century, this accommodation appears to have become too limited for the growing power of the first Lord Ruthven, but instead of adding to it in the usual manner, he built another independent tower to the west, close by. This was an L-shaped structure of roughly the same appearance as the first, but with the wing rising a storey higher—seen on the left of the sketch. These two towers had no communication with each other, except by a sort of wooden bridge from battlement to battlement—a highly unusual and inconvenient arrangement. Presumably the idea was a sort of insurance policy; if the castle was besieged, and one tower was taken, the defenders could still retire over the bridge, remove it behind them, and the besiegers would have to begin all over again. The Ruthvens must have been anticipating trouble —which is not surprising, for they were a turbulent lot, as history proved. Towards the end of the 16th century, when noblemen began to be a little more interested in comfort and style, as distinct from mere defence, the space between the two towers was filled in by a connecting link of building, and Ruthven Castle came to look as it does now. This latest portion rose only to three storeys, with a long sloping roof. It contained a timber stair to serve both towers.

The ground floor of the original tower is the only vaulted

apartment. In the second L-shaped part, the stair does not rise in the wing, as might be expected, but in a slightly projecting semi-circular turret to the north-west (not seen in sketch). This second building had its entrance at first floor level, reached by a removable wooden stair—quite a common device in unsettled times.

The building is now in the care of the Ministry of Works.

An interesting feature of Huntingtower is the manner in which the parapet and rounds at its angles were partly roofed-in, to form a covered passage to apartments in the garrets.

This was the scene of the famous 'Raid of Ruthven' in 1582, when the fourth Lord Ruthven, who had been created first Earl of Gowrie, and some other Protestant nobles, kidnapped the fifteen-year-old King James Sixth, and brought him prisoner to hold him here for nearly a year. In those days the men who held the King ruled the land, and this the Ruthven raiders proceeded to do in very rough fashion. Eventually James achieved his freedom, and though he was not strong enough to move drastically against those who had injured him, the Ruthven lords were banished to England.

Twenty years later, the Gowrie Conspiracy, implicating members of the same family, spelt the end of the Ruthvens—although it is now thought that it was largely a belatedly revengeful plot by the King himself, and the young Earl of Gowrie and his brother the Master of Ruthven, the innocent victims of James's hatred. At anyrate, the Ruthvens died, their name was proscribed, and their lands forfeited. Thus it was that the new Murray owners changed the name to Huntingtower.

CASTLE HUNTLY

In 1452, Andrew, first Lord Gray of Fowlis, received royal license to build this fortalice, and chose for site a dramatic volcanic rock that thrusts up out of the fertile levels of the Carse of Gowrie, just south of Longforgan and seven miles west of Dundee. The massive and lofty tower that he built thereafter still romantically dominates the plain. How it gained its name is a mystery; no proud Lord Gray was likely to call his castle after distant 'in-laws', however notable, merely because a later female member of his family married one of the Huntly Gordons. Yet the place seems to have been so-called from the first.

The building is essentially an L-planned tower of the 15th century, that has been considerably altered in the 17th and 18th centuries and later. Its 10-foot thick red sandstone walls are so well integrated with the naked rock of its foundations that it is difficult to ascertain at what level rock ends and masonry begins. Originally there appears to have been three main floors above the level of the top of the rock, with a pit of prison dug out of the solid rock below, but in the 17th century an extra floor was contrived. The pit was a fearsome place—its tiny window-slit is the lowermost aperture seen in the sketch—reached only by a trap-door in the floor of the guardroom above. Into this guard-room was the original entrance of the castle, in the re-entrant, now covered over by later building. The main block at this level consisted of three vaulted cellars, part cut into the living rock. A well, now filled in, was sunk in the floor of one.

Access to the main living floors above has been most unusual —and inconvenient—in the cause of security. There was no permanent internal stair at this level, only a passage high in the springing of the guardroom vault, which would be reached by a removable ladder which could be pulled up. This seems to have been the only approach to the living quarters originally.

The hall on the first floor measured 43 by 19 feet, with a high barrel vault; this vault was removed by the third Earl of King-horne, however, in the 17th century, and the extra floor inserted. The upper floors have also since been somewhat altered and sub-divided, but the many wall-closets and garderobes remain. The stair to these upper floors was a turnpike in the thickness of the walling.

The top storey of this lofty tower, no less than 116 feet above the level Carse, was altogether altered in appearance at the end of the 18th century, when the sham angle-turrets and battlements and the windowed caphouse were added, much detracting from the authentic aspect of the whole. New building was at the same time added to the east, wherein lies the modern doorway, and also within the re-entrant. Above this, still more unsightly, has recently been added a brick-built erection, quite out-of-keeping with the dignified ancient work.

The castle remained in the possession of the Grays until 1614. During this period the family produced some of the ablest and at the same time worst characters in our history. Andrew, second Lord, Justice General of Scotland, an intimate of James Third, betrayed that monarch to the usurping Albany, and then Albany to the young James Fourth. Patrick, fourth Lord, treasonably surrendered Broughty Castle to the invading English. But it was his grandson, Patrick, sixth Lord, who as Master of Gray, over-shadowed all others by his treachery. Undoubtedly he was one of the most gifted, shrewdest and most blackguardly characters in Scots history—and the handsomest man in Europe of his day. His son sold the castle to the 11th Lord Glamis and first Earl of Kinghorne.

KELTIE CASTLE

Standing fairly high amongst the rolling northern foothills of the Ochils, within a fine wooded estate, and about a mile west of Dunning, Keltie is a small but sturdy and most attractive laird's house, dating substantially, apparently, from the end of the 16th century, but which may well incorporate still older work. Inset over the doorway is the former pediment of a dormer window, dated 1600. This date fairly well suits the general style of the building as it now stands. Certainly MacGibbon and Ross, in their monumental and excellent work, *The Castellated and Domestic Architecture of Scotland*, are mistaken when they ascribe the building of this house to John Drummond of Keltie, who was served heir of his father in 1699. They offer as authority for this the fact that one of the lintels bears the initials J.D. and M.C., and is dated 1712. Most obviously however the style of the structure belongs to more than a century earlier. No doubt this inscription relates merely to some alteration. MacGibbon and Ross may be forgiven this slip, for they admit that they did not visit the house for themselves, but were indebted to someone else for the details.

Keltie is a fairly plain building on the L-plan, the main block lying east and west, with a slightly taller wing, in which is the doorway, projecting to the south. This looks like a typical stair-tower, but in fact the stair does not rise here, but nearby. There are three storeys and a garret beneath a steep roof, though this has apparently been lowered, but only slightly; no doubt the gables were originally crowstepped in the usual fashion, and the attic windows provided with triangular pediments. There is a most unusual and attractive turret corbelled out on the east gable above first-floor level, as seen in sketch. This is neither circular, nor with the conical roof that is normal, nor is it set in the usual position, at eaves level. It has a lean-to roof, with crow-stepped half-gable, and is provided with two little windows and no fewer than five shot-holes. A most interesting feature. There are other shot-holes elsewhere, and a stout iron grille, or yett, is still in position over a first-floor window in the west gable.

Internally, the house is equally attractive. The ground floor is not vaulted. The kitchen is here, with traces of the original great arched fireplace visible in the east gable. This, as is quite common, had a window at the back of the in-going. The turnpike stair leads to the fine Hall on the first floor, which has had a wall-chamber to the south. At this level, in the west gable, there is a garderobe with shute. Above is the usual bedroom accommodation.

When forming a bathroom on an upper floor some time ago, it is reported that a woman's skeleton was found walled-up in the masonry.

From at least the early 15th century until 1692 Keltie belonged to the family of Bonar, which also had possessed the lands of Forgandenny, Invermay and Kilgraston nearby. William Bonar de Keltie witnessed a charter in 1454 in which a perpetual liberty to fish for eels in the place commonly called Polpefery is granted to the Abbot and Convent of Inchaffery, on condition that they prayed for the granter's soul, and that of his wife Janet and his heir Alexander. Could this possibly be conscience asserting itself, and relating to the walled-up lady?

In 1649 Cromwell valued William Bonar 'for Keltie and pendicles 5 hundredth fourscore pounds'.

Master John Drummond, a scion of the family of Culdees and minister of Monzie, uncle of the John Drummond mentioned earlier, purchased Keltie in 1692, and this family retained possession until 1812 when an heiress married the 8th Earl of Airlie.

This pleasant fortalice is particularly interesting in that it stands today as it was built, with no additions and extensions, excellently maintained in the appreciative care of its present tenant.

KINNAIRD CASTLE

This tall and impressive tower, once a roofless ruin but restored towards the close of last century and again inhabited, stands in a commanding situation on a spur of the Sidlaw foothills overlooking the Carse of Gowrie, ten miles west of Dundee.

It seems to be a plain fortalice of the 15th century, though possibly earlier, oblong on plan with a small projecting tower or buttress at the south-west angle. This is a remarkable feature, for it is not a stair-tower as it would seem, although to some extent it covers and strengthens the stair-well which rises just behind it. Tiny chambers are contrived within its thickness at first, second and third floor levels; otherwise it is merely a glorified buttress, its summit forming a little watch-tower—a unique provision, in my experience, although there is something rather like it at Drummond Castle, also in Perthshire.

The building, which has formerly had a courtyard or outer bailey to the west, rises four storeys to the parapet, sixty feet above ground level, and there is a gabled garret storey above, within the parapet-walk. This parapet is provided with machicolated projections at various points, for the dropping of missiles upon unwelcome guests below. There is also a peculiar semi-octagonal open 'round' at the south-eastern angle; usually these are circular, of course.

There are two entrances, both in the south front. One is at basement level, with an arched doorway protected by an iron yett; the other at first floor in the buttress tower, now reached by a stone forestair. Originally almost certainly this door would give access to a parapet-walk which would run round the top of the walling of the courtyard, about 15 feet above ground level. Its outer door, of wood, apparently was raised and lowered outwards from a floor hinge, to form a sort of drawbridge when down—the sockets for which are still to be seen.

The ground floor chamber is very unusual in that it is vaulted only at the ends and not in the centre, where a timber ceiling has been supported on corbels—again something that I have not come across elsewhere. There is an unpleasant pit cut here, in the solid rock of the site, 18 feet deep and 4½ feet in diameter, presumably a dungeon of horrible dimensions since it is not a well. Another dungeon is excavated in the masonry of the buttress basement.

The stair rises within the thickness of the wall, to the left of the doorway, of the straight variety as far as the first floor. Here is the Hall, with a large mural chamber reached from the stairway, two windows with stone seats, and a mural-closet with drain. The same pattern is continued above, the stair now being the usual turnpike, rising within the walling of the south-west angle, each floor being well provided with mural chambers and garderobes.

To the east of the tower, close but not actually attached thereto, is a small two-storeyed 17th century building, containing a later kitchen with an enormous arched fireplace 13½ feet wide by 6 deep. There is a sort of service window at the end of the kitchen nearest the tower—presumably for victuals to be pushed through for the laird's household. A dormer window of the upper chamber is inscribed P.T. 11 M.O. and dated 1610. The Sir Patrick Threipland, first baronet of Fingask nearby, who bought this estate from previous owners, is not supposed to have done so until 1674, two years after acquiring Fingask itself. It would be interesting to know how this window comes to be dated 1610.

Kinnaird was the original seat of the noble family of that name, who it is said built their castle here in the 13th century—though this is too early for any of the present buildings. James Sixth visited Kinnaird for eight days hunting in 1716.

TOWER OF LETHENDY

At first glance Lethendy appears to be only a typical imposing late Victorian mansion in the 'Scottish Baronial' style, set in pleasant fruit-growing land four miles south-west of Blairgowrie. But closer inspection, to the rear, reveals a more modest and simple L-planned house of three storeys and a garret, dating from the late 16th or early 17th century, built of the same local red sandstone, on to which the modern mansion is grafted.

This early house has itself suffered some alterations, but the main features survive. Formerly it would appear much taller than it does today; it is dwarfed by the modern work, and the ground level has obviously been raised considerably, especially to the south. There seems to have been trouble with the foundations and site at various periods; the main block has been strengthened by an extra thickness of walling up to first-floor level at both sides, and to the south two great buttresses have been added at some later date—a striking and unusual feature. The entire southern gable has been refaced.

The doorway was in the east front, now covered by modern building, defended by a splayed gunloop. Above was a panel bearing the arms of Heron and reputedly the date 1678. The old kitchen occupies the east end of the vaulted main block basement. A scale-and-platt staircase rises in the wing, with underneath a narrow vaulted pit.

From a daughter of Heron of Lethendy descended Graham of Claverhouse, Bonnie Dundee.

PITTHEAVLIS CASTLE

Here is a very typical and attractive tower-house of the late 16th century, rising impressively above its numerous modern neighbours in a suburb only a mile west of the centre of Perth. Although it has lost its surrounding lands, the house is still in occupation and in good condition.

The building is L-planned, the substantial main block rising to three storeys and a garret. The projecting stair-tower is, as is unusual, slightly lower.

The entrance is in the foot of the stair-tower guarded by a splayed gunloop, and each of the two angle-turrets that crown this tower are also provided with gunloops.

The handsome and massive chimney-stack rising in the centre of the south front is a notable feature.

Pittheavlis is distinctly unusual in apparently having escaped the attentions of historians, local and national. Presumably nothing ever happened here of sufficient importance or excitement to chronicle, despite—or possibly even because of—the sturdy strength and amplitude of gunloops. In 1586 a charter confirms the sale of these lands by John Ross of Craigie—a larger property nearby—to Robert Stewart. This date well matches the style of architecture. This Stewart laird, if the builder, cannot have remained long in possession, for by 1636 we find Patrick, son of Laurence Oliphant of Bachilton served heir in the lands and quarry of Pittheavlis.

METHVEN CASTLE

Magnificently sited on the summit of a ridge facing south over a wide prospect, five miles west of Perth, Methven dates mainly from the first half of the 17th century, although undoubtedly older work is incorporated. As it stands, it represents handsomely almost the last stage in the development of fortified house into impressive mansion. Almost the only true defensive feature I could find was a shot-hole in the north-west tower protecting the entrance.

The building is almost square on plan, having round towers with unusual ogee roofs rising at each angle, containing stairs, with later, lower additions to east and west. The walls, of good coursed red rubble, rise to four storeys and a garret. The windows are larger and more regular than in earlier fortalices—and internally the rooms are regularly planned, numerous, spacious and well-dimensioned. None are vaulted.

The doorway, covered by a modern porch, was in the centre of the double-gabled north front, and above it, at roof-level, is a small balustraded parapet and platform, drained by cannon-spouts; it can be seen how the defensive crenellated parapet has now been reduced to this purely decorative function.

Methven has had a stirring history, being for long intimately connected with the royal house of Stewart. Prior to 1323 the lands belonged to the great Norman family of Mowbray. Sir Roger Mowbray however took the wrong side during the Wars of Independence, supporting Baliol and the English interest. The Bruce therefore confiscated his lands and bestowed them on his own son-in-law Walter, the 8th High Steward of Scotland, whose son of course succeeded to the throne as Robert Second in 1371. By him the lordship of Methven was granted to his own second son, Walter Stewart, Earl of Atholl. He was forfeited however, and Methven remained with the Crown for a consider-able time, being generally used as a dower-house for the Queens-Dowager. James Fourth settled Methven on Margaret Tudor his English bride, who, widowed after Flodden, eventually married another Stewart, a descendant of Robert Second also. She procured for this third husband the title of Lord Methven in 1528. She died at Methven Castle in 1540. Lord Methven after-wards married Janet Stewart, daughter of the Earl of Atholl, and their son became second lord, being killed by a cannon-ball from Edinburgh Castle in 1572, leaving Henry, third lord, who died without issue and the property reverted to the Crown. In 1584 the lordship was granted by James Sixth to his favourite and distant cousin Esmé Stewart, Seigneur D'Aubigny, whom he made Chancellor and first Duke of Lennox. The second Duke, Ludovick, was all his life a great friend of James, and he it was who presumably built most of the castle as it now stands, which would account for its size and excellence. It was purchased from the last Duke in 1664 by Patrick Smythe of Braco. His great-grandson, David Smythe, assumed the title of Lord Methven on appointment as a Senator of the College of Justice. It remained with his successors until recent times.

MEGGERNIE CASTLE

This attractive fortalice, dating probably from the 16th century, although possibly incorporating a still older nucleus, has one or two rather unusual features. A large and more modern mansion has been attached. It stands about half-way up what has been described as the longest glen in Scotland—the romantic and lovely Glen Lyon—and is embosomed in an estate of magnificent old trees, largely planted by one of the Menzies lairds in the 18th century. Its lime avenue is said to be the finest in the land.

The original building consists of an almost square tall tower, five storeys in height, steep-roofed, and embellished with square corner-turrets corbelled out at the angles. It is unusual to find all the turrets square. The walls reaching five feet in thickness, are harled and whitewashed, and stand out notably against the enclosing green hillsides. Certain of the windows have shot-holes below their sills. The door is in the centre of the south front, and admits to a vaulted basement. The normal arrangement of Hall on first floor and sleeping accommodation above would formerly apply.

Despite the commonly held belief that Glen Lyon was Campbell territory, after they had driven out the MacGregors, a considerable part of the glen was in fact held by the great Perthshire clan of Menzies, and Meggernie was a stronghold of Menzies of Culdares. The most famous member of this line was 'Old Culdares', the great sylviculturalist. He was noted for more than his vast tree-planting activities, however, greatly admired as this has been. He was 'out' in the Jacobite Rising in 1715, and taken prisoner at the Battle of Preston. The government of the day seems to have been fairly lenient with the young man, however, and he did not suffer so greatly as many. Perhaps that was why he did not take an active part in the later Rising of 1745—although *anno domini* itself may have had a lot to do with it. But if he did not go campaigning, he did not remain entirely quiescent either; indeed he played an extraordinary double game, ostensibly loyal to the government but by no means wholly failing the cause he had at heart. He is said to have presented Prince Charles with a handsome charger, and more important, after Culloden, to have sheltered on his lands many Jacobite fugitives, while at the same time hospitably entertaining the Redcoat soldiers sent to hunt them down.

'Old Culdares'' son left no male heir, and the property was inherited by Stewart of Cardney, who, with his successors, adopted the name of Stewart-Menzies. They retained possession of the estate until it was sold in 1885.

One account claims that Meggernie Castle was built in 1579, and goes on to say that it was erected as the seat of Sir John Stewart, son of King Robert the Second—which of course is manifestly ridiculous. Robert Second died in 1390. Nothing about the castle gives the impression of so early a date as the 14th century; indeed 1579 seems entirely suitable to the style of architecture. There may have been an earlier castle on the site. There appears no reason to doubt that the present building was the work of its Menzies lairds.

Meggernie is reputed to be haunted, on fairly substantial evidence, by the top half of a sadly beautiful lady. She is said to be the wife of an early Menzies laird who murdered her in a fit of insane jealousy, and then cut her body in halves for easier and more secret disposal, seeming to have more difficulty in getting rid of the upper than the lower half. The tradition is that the wretched man was himself murdered later on—but it is the poor lady who haunts the turret-room of Meggernie.

MEGGINCH CASTLE

The ancient house of Megginch, for so long the home of a branch of the Drummond family, stands amidst timbered policies in the fertile Carse of Gowrie almost midway between Perth and Dundee. Presumably this description of its surroundings did not apply in the distant days when it got its name, for Megginch or Melginch, is supposed to be a corruption of the Gaelic *Maol-inch*, the Barren or Bald Island—the island referring no doubt to firm ground amongst marshlands, for the castle lies fully a mile inland from the Tay. If these were then the topographical conditions, they would certainly give the fortalice a defensive strength not apparent today.

Megginch is an attractive building of warm red sandstone, dating substantially from the 16th century, but which has been much altered and greatly added to in the early 19th century. The north front is largely unaltered, but unfortunately most of the interesting features are not at that side, and it was very difficult to find a position from which to make any sketch to show these features.

The original building has been a simple oblong main block of three storeys and a garret, with a circular stair-tower projecting on the south front. As is usual, this round tower is built out to the square at the top to form a watch-chamber, but the style of the corbelling is unusual, as is the most peculiar stair-turret and caphouse combined, which gives access to this watch-chamber, as seen in sketch. There are two conical-roofed corner-turrets at either end of the main block, connected by a parapet which is interrupted by the stair-tower. Obviously the entire upper storey of the castle has been altered at this period, probably at the end of the 16th century—so that the lower parts of the building may well be considerably older. This is indicated by the presence of plentiful wide splayed gunloops at ground level, these seeming to be of an earlier period than those on the upper works. The window levels have been much changed also, indicating very comprehensive internal re-arrangement.

Over one of the windows is inscribed PETRUS HAY AEDIFICIUM EXTRUXIT AN 1575, and this date well matches with the upper features and early alterations.

The first of the Hay lairds, also Peter, was a son of Hay of

Leys, an ancient family connected with the chiefly house of Erroll. He died before 1496, and may well have been the builder of the original castle, which was altered in 1575 by his namesake mentioned above. The last of the Hays of Megginch, Sir George, sold the property to John Drummond, 8th feudal baron of Lennoch, Hereditory Seneschal of Strathearn. The third Drummond of Megginch was the first member for Perthshire of the newly-formed and unpopular united Parliament in London, after the Union of 1707. He seems to have been firmly on the side of entrenched authority, unlike other members of the Drummond clan, for he is also reported as being strong in his attempts to hunt down Rob Roy MacGregor when the latter was outlawed. His son Adam lived elsewhere, and when a nephew John eventually succeeded to Megginch he complained that it was in a bad state with 'the doos in all the rooms'. Later lairds were prominent in other walks of life, Sir Adam being a noted admiral at the end of the 18th century, and his brother General Sir Gordon a foremost commander during the American War of Independence.

It is good to know that Megginch is still the home of the Drummonds, in days when so few ancient houses remain in the possession of the families historically linked with them.

CASTLE MENZIES

Standing in parkland at the base of steeply rising Weem Hill about a mile west of Aberfeldy, this is a particularly large and commodious mansion for its period, long the seat of the chiefs of Clan Menzies. Of late years, along with its still larger modern extension, it has been unoccupied and fallen on evil days, and it looked as though it was fated to crumble to complete ruin. Fortunately, however, the Clan Menzies Society has come to its rescue, and intends to preserve at least the original part of the house as a clan centre.

The early building dates from the second half of the 16th century, and belongs to the Z-plan, consisting of a substantial main block of three storeys and an attic, with square towers containing five storeys projecting at opposite corners. Most of the angles are crowned by circular-turrets, and the walling is well furnished with gunloops and heraldic decoration. The original entrance lies in the re-entrant at the foot of the south-west tower, guarded by gunloops, and with a heraldic panel above bearing the arms of James Menzies and Barbara Stewart, daughter of the Earl of Atholl. The elaborate porch and doorway in the centre of the main block is of later date.

The ground floor is vaulted, with the Hall, a handsome room on the first floor, sharing the main block with a private chamber to the east. The stair rises in the south-west tower. There has certainly been ample domestic accommodation above, though insufficient apparently for later Menzies lairds, for they built the very large extensions to north and west in 1840 and later, fortunately in the same style of architecture.

One of the dormer pediments is dated 1577 and bears the initials I.M.B. presumably for James and Barbara Menzies, followed by the legend IN.OWR.TYME and on the lintel PRYSIT BE GOD FOR EVER.

The original Menzies seat was at Comrie Castle nearby (not to be confused with Comrie in upper Strathearn). This was destroyed by fire in 1487—whether accidentally or otherwise is not clear. The then laird, Sir Robert Menzies thereafter built a new house known as The Place of Weem, on the present site. Scarcely was he settled into his new establishment, however, than Stewart of Garth and others of that clan, with whom Menzies was at feud, descended upon him and demolished the house. Sir Robert was in good odour with King James Fourth, and managed to obtain a royal decree of compensation for wrongs done him—but the King's writ does not seem to have run strongly in upland Perthshire, for he apparently got nothing out of the offenders. A long legal battle ensued, productive of little but costs no doubt. Sir Robert's great grandson James, however, perceived the better way. He ended the feud and won peace and presumably much prosperity too, by wooing and marrying no less than the Lady Barbara, daughter of the Stewart Earl of Atholl himself, as above mentioned, and thereafter was able to build this splendid mansion.

The family obtained a baronetcy of Nova Scotia in 1665. Although the Menzies chief himself was not involved in the Rising of 1745, the family were Jacobite, and the clan was 'out' under Menzies of Shian. The chief's prudence evidently did not prevent him from showing hospitality to the contender for the Stuart cause, for Prince Charlie's room is still pointed out at Castle Menzies.

To the Menzies family Scotland owes the introduction of the larch tree, the first saplings of which were raised by Menzies of Culdares in Glen Lyon nearby.

MONZIE CASTLE

Lying at the foot of the Knock Hill of Crieff, to the north, within a large estate, Monzie is a small and attractive early 17th-century house to which a vast mansion in the pseudo-castellated style was added in the early 19th century. Fortunately this great addition has been effected all at one side, so that although the modern work much overshadows the old, the original house still stands almost unaltered externally, and contrasts with the other most notably in its authentic simplicity.

The early building is an L-planned structure, rubble-built, plain but with some interesting features. It is two storeys and an attic in height, steep-roofed, with dormer windows and crow-stepped gables, but without turrets or stair-tower. There is, however, just the merest suspicion of external projection built out above first floor level in the re-entrant angle, to indicate where the upper turnpike stairway, now removed, has risen.

The good moulded doorway is in the wing, within the re-entrant, and bears above it the date 1634, with a heraldic panel depicting the arms of Campbell and Graham. A circular shot-hole protects this doorway, in the main block, and there is another of the same type, placed in a rather unusual position, at first-floor level in the south gable.

The door opens into a lobby from which a squared scale-and-platt stair rises. This appears to be original as far as the first floor, but now continues higher, replacing the smaller turnpike stair in the angle, already mentioned. The ground floor is not vaulted, and may never have been so—although there has been considerable reconstruction internally, especially following a serious fire. The Hall, now subdivided, formerly occupied the entire first floor of the main block, and is a handsome room, pleasingly panelled, with a great arched fireplace at its south end. The heraldic decoration of the lintel of this has been renewed, but the date 1634 here seems to be authentic.

There are garderobes in the thickness of the walling of the west wing, at both first and second floor levels, the former being provided with a drain in the floor. These wall chambers give the impression of older work than the first half of the 17th century, and may well represent an earlier fortalice on the same site.

A most intriguing and unusual feature of this charming house

[138]

is the large number of sundials. Indeed almost every window jamb is provided with one, something that I have never seen elsewhere. It would be interesting to know the reason for this preoccupation with the passing hour on the part of the builder of Monzie.

The property was a Campbell holding from fairly early times, and was given by Sir Duncan Campbell of Glenorchy, ancestor of the great Breadalbane family, to his fifth son, Archibald, by his wife, the Lady Jane Stewart, daughter of the Earl of Atholl, in the 16th century. Accordingly there may well be older work incorporated in the present building. Monzie remained with the descendants of this family until 1869.

Happily the house is in excellent condition, the interior having been most skilfully restored by the expert Sir Robert Lorimer, who so greatly loved these fortalices. Happily, too, the present proprietor is most appreciative and concerned for the ancient building's preservation.

MURTHLY CASTLE

Standing deep in a large estate about four miles east of Dunkeld, near the south bank of Tay, Murthly Castle is an interesting building of many periods. From the front, or eastern aspect, it is almost impossible to distinguish the various periods of construction, apart from the topmost turrets and dormers of the original tower, so intermingled are they. But from the rear, or western viewpoint, the older work becomes much more readily identifiable, as in sketch. The whole now forms three sides of a square, and represents extensions to an original small free-standing tower of fairly early date, that stands at the south-west angle of the courtyard, almost square in plan but with a slight projection at its south-east corner to accommodate the turnpike stair. The date of this early keep, like that of Grantully to which it has been allied throughout its history, is uncertain, but its upper storeys were altered probably towards the end of the 16th century when the angle-turrets were added and the first extensions made. One of these extensions seems to have been another plain gabled tower to the south-east, linked by later building. Still larger extensions were made when Murthly came into the possession of the Stewarts of Grantully in 1615, and later. Numerous carved dormer pediments of various dates in the 17th century are built into the walling of these later additions. A central and decorative classical style entrance-hall and exterior stone stairway was finally contrived, to partly fill the open square of the courtyard.

The early tower, said to have been a hunting seat of the Scottish kings, is four storeys and an attic in height, and rubble-built. Its angle-turrets are interesting in being adorned with stringcourses and provided with quatrefoil gunloops. Another peculiarity is the little ornamental corbelled-out projection like another tiny angle-turret at the north-west angle, obviously original—something that I have not noted elsewhere. Near roof-level on the east front is a heraldic panel, somewhat worn, bearing the arms of Stewart and a 17th century date that is probably 1617. A tall and substantial chimney-stack rises on this front.

The building is in excellent condition, and still occupied. To the south is a very fine walled garden, laid out in 1669, in the Dutch fashion, with terraces, pools and clipped hedges.

A great new castle was designed and erected nearby by Gillespie

Graham the famous architect, in the 19th century, in Elizabethan style, for the 6th baronet. It was never completed.

The Stewarts of Grantully and Murthly descend from Alexander, 4th High Steward of Scotland by a younger son, Sir John Stewart of Bonkyl—from whom also derive the houses of Lennox, D'Aubigny and Darnley, and therefore James Sixth and the later Stuart kings, and also Appin and Galloway amongst others. The baronetcy conferred in 1683 became extinct with the 8th baronet in 1890.

NEWTON CASTLE, BLAIRGOWRIE

In a lofty position on high ground above the town, and over-looking the wide vale of Strathmore, this handsome old fortalice was once the seat of the lords of the barony of Blairgowrie. It is said to be built on the site of a still older castle; indeed, there is a legend that the earlier stronghold was burned and destroyed by Cromwell, but this would seem to be incorrect, for the house as it now stands is typical of a period about half a century earlier than Cromwell. The invading Protector may indeed have done some burning here, but if so it was presumably *this* house that he sought to destroy, not its predecessor—and evidently less than successfully. The tradition runs that a number of gentlemen who had been defending it, took refuge in one of the vaults, semi-subterranean, and when the fire was over, emerged un-scathed, thanks to its depth and thick walling.

The house, built on a slanting site, conforms to a variation of the Z-plan, having a main block of three storeys and an attic running east and west, with a square stair-tower rising at the south-east angle and a round one at the north-west, this latter being corbelled out to the square to form a watch-chamber in its top storey. The original door is in the foot of the square stair-tower, and is protected by a splayed gunloop. The walls are white-washed, and the gables crowstepped. On the east front, not seen in sketch, wherein is the present front door, there is a tiny stair-turret corbelled out above second floor level, the lowest corbel of which is fashioned in the form of a human face—some-thing that I have not seen in such a position elsewhere.

Internally there has been some alteration and modernisation, as is to be expected, but the ground floor vaulting and a certain amount of 17th-century panelling remains. The usual arrange-ment of Hall on first floor and domestic accommodation higher would prevail.

Newton belonged to a branch of the Drummond family, of Stobhall and Cargill, not far away. Here was born in 1687 George Drummond who was to achieve fame in a number of directions. He became prominent in the government service and was appointed Accountant-General of the Customs—no doubt in return for the help he gave the politicians who negotiated the Treaty of Union in 1707, of which he was a strong protagonist young as he was. Contrary to the sympathies of most of the Drummond clan, he was hostile to the Jacobite cause, and actually fought at the Battle of Sheriffmuir in the Rising of 1715 against the Stuart arms, in which the Drummond cavalry was prominent on the other side. Drummond of Megginch was likewise on the government side, of course. George Drummond was Lord Provost of Edinburgh no less than six times, and it is after him that Drummond Place and other Edinburgh streets are named. He helped to found the Royal Infirmary and also the Royal Exchange of the capital, and was instrumental in getting five professorships set up at the University there. Altogether a remarkable man, and no doubt a patriot, however much many of his kinsmen may have doubted it.

His birthplace is today a most attractive house, occupied and in good repair, standing in a pleasant garden. The Green Lady who is reputed to haunt it could scarcely have chosen a less ominous-seeming refuge.

NEWTON HOUSE, DOUNE

Standing high above the Ardoch Water on the eastern outskirts of Doune, and just across from the imposing ruined fortress of Doune Castle, this pleasant house appears to date from the second half of the 16th century, and in contrast to its huge neighbour, is still occupied. It is a fairly typical L-planned fortalice, with a stair-turret corbelled out in the re-entrant above first floor level, and otherwise fairly plain. It has one unusual feature, however; the wing of the L while still in fact a wing and not a tower, is rounded, with a semi-circular crowstepped gable—an architectural construction seldom seen.

A lower and later wing was an early addition to the west.

The walls, harled and pink-washed, are four storeys and a garret in height. The original entrance, as usual, is in the re-entrant and gives access to the wide turnpike stair which rises only to the first floor, the ascent being continued by the turret-stair. A short flight of straight steps leads down into the semi-subterranean vaulted basement, in which are traces of a built-up gunloop for protecting the entrance. At door level is the old kitchen, still with wide arched fireplace, though this is now filled in and the chamber used as dining-room.

The Hall is on the first floor, the old access to it being built up and a lobby formed by shortening the room to the east. A door communicates with the first floor of the western addition. Above are two more storeys, those in the wing, above the main stairway being on a slightly different level.

A garderobe or wall-closet opens off the main bedroom above the Hall, and there are some good moulded fireplaces.

A courtyard has extended to west and south, part of the arched gateway to which remains against the addition walling.

This very attractive house, built so close to the mighty Doune Castle, clearly had some connection therewith, for great lords like the Earls of Moray did not permit lesser lairds to build fortalices directly under their windows. Newton was in fact the residence of the Edmonstone family, who became apparently hereditary captains or keepers of Doune Castle. In the Register of the Great Seal we read that in 1538 the King granted to 'his own familiar servitor, James Edmonstoun, son natural of the deceased William Edmonstoun of Duntreath, knight, the lands of Newton of Doune . . . moreover he hath revoked the charter of feuferme . . . formerly granted to James Stewart, Captain of Doune.'

The Edmonstones of Newton remained loyal to the royal Stewarts, as well as to the Stewarts of Doune and Moray, and in 1708 the laird of Newton was one of five Perthshire lairds arrested in an abortive attempt to place the Old Pretender on the throne. They were taken to London, but sent back to Edinburgh for trial. Happily the prosecution failed because of gross mishandling by the Lord Advocate, and Edmonstone and his friends were released.

It is interesting to note that on 13th September 1745, at nearby Doune Lodge, now a seat of the Earl of Moray, Prince Charlie 'pree'd the mou' of Miss Robina Edmonstone. The last of the line was Miss Grizzel Edmonstone who died in 1852. Her cousin sold the property to John Campbell, a Glasgow merchant in 1858. The present laird is General Campbell.

STOBHALL

Stobhall, once known also as Stobshaw, set impressively on a high tongue of ridge above the Tay some nine miles north of Perth, is one of the most unusual and interesting houses in this county. Unlike the vast majority of its kind, it consists not of a tower, keep, or main block, with or without extensions, but of a loose group of no fewer than four unconnected buildings, all placed at odd angles and levels, dictated by the broken and uneven site, although all within an irregular courtyard wall. The effect is very striking, giving an impression almost ecclesiastical rather than baronially defensive—an illusion that is heightened by the fact that the major portion of the largest and most central building is a chapel. It has been suggested, however, that this edifice was originally the banqueting hall.

The castle is entered, from the west, by a picturesque arched passage or pend beside a long two-storeyed block, with good dormer windows and steep crowstepped roof, the building commenced apparently by John Drummond, 2nd Earl of Perth in the early 17th century. In this house was a large kitchen and parlour, with bedroom accommodation above. It was used as the dower-house for Drummond Castle. The arms of the Earl and his Countess, Lady Jane Kerr, daughter of the Earl of Roxburghe, are carved over the entrance.

In the centre of the courtyard is the Chapel block, as illustrated. It is a tall L-shaped building of the late 16th century, containing both the chapel premises and a dwelling house. This latter rises to three storeys and an attic, with a two-storeyed angle-turret crowning the south-west corner. There is a strengthening plinth of masonry at ground level to the south-east, where the site tends to fall away. This block was erected by David, second Lord Drummond, whose arms and initials are inscribed on the outside, with the date 1578. The chapel has a fine tempera painted ceiling, with a series of equestrian figures representing the kings of the earth. Owing to the adherence of the Perth family to the Old Faith, Roman Catholic services were held in this chapel during the 17th century by special permission when forbidden elsewhere in Scotland.

Next to the Chapel block is the two-storeyed Laundry building, with brew-house and bakehouse, and further to the east is another

[146]

domestic range that comprised kitchen and storehouse. These are both later buildings.

There must have been much earlier buildings on the strong defensive site, for the Drummonds had been settled here from as early as the 14th century, when Bruce granted the barony to Sir Malcolm Drummond after Bannockburn. Sir Malcolm it was who so greatly assisted that victory by advising the use of caltrops, or three-pointed iron spikes strewn on the ground, to cripple the English horses. His great-granddaughter Annabella Drummond became the queen of Robert Third.

Stobhall was the principal seat of the Drummonds until Sir John, 12th in descent from the founder, was created first Lord Drummond in 1487, and he it was who a year later began the building of Drummond Castle near Crieff, and moved thereto, twenty miles away. After being a dower-house for widows of former lords, Stobhall became for long the estate factor's house. However, thanks to a comparatively recent and happy arrangement, though the Earl of Ancaster still owns Drummond Castle, heired through the forfeiture of the main line for their Jacobite sympathies, the present head of the Drummond family, the reigning Earl of Perth, is once again installed at Stobhall.

[147]

WILLIAMSTOUN

This most interesting and unusual little 17th-century mansion, now a farmhouse, is situated on a ridge between the Cowgask Burn and the Pow Water, in the Findo Gask area of Strathearn about one mile east of Madderty. The building conforms to a variation of the T-plan, with a circular tower projecting from an oblong main block on the north front, but not in the centre of it, corbelled out to the square to form a watch-chamber above. This little apartment is reached by a tiny stair built out in a small squat turret in the north-west re-entrant angle. It certainly seems a lot of trouble to have gone to, this building of a watch-chamber and its elaborate access, when, with no great height to it, an ordinary attic in the roof would probably have served just as well—for there are no other defensive features about the house, and it is only two storeys and a garret in height—unusually low for the period.

Other unusual features are the lack of crowstepping on the gables; the somewhat elaborate chimney-stacks; the planing away of the masonry to the left of the window under the stair-turret, to give a better field of view; and the fact that the entrance is not here, in the re-entrant angle as might be expected, but round at the opposite side of the house, in the centre of the south front. Nearby rises a very massive chimney-stack, from ground level, of fine proportions. The main stairway is exceptional too, in that it is neither turnpike nor squared scale-and-platt, but rises straight from the front door to the first floor, the rooms opening off on either hand, a very modern conception.

The fact is, of course, that, delightful as it may be, Williamstoun is really neither one thing nor another. It belongs to the very end of the defensive period, when the need for fortifying one's house was deemed to have passed away—lairds not foreseeing the Jacobite Risings of a hundred years later—but when the traditional *style* of building was still considered to be necessary for a country gentleman's dignity. In this house, therefore, the north front is that of a fortalice, and the south that of an ordinary country house of later years.

There have been certain minor modernisations to the east of the north front, as hinted at in sketch, but these have but little interfered with the original aspect.

The entire building is in excellent condition, and lovingly cared for.

The lands seem to have been purchased and the house built about the middle of the 17th century, by Sir Laurence Oliphant of Gask nearby, for his eldest son, who married and desired to set up house during the lifetime of his father. There is more in this than meets the eye—and a romantic story it makes, according to the Gask charter-chest, which says that 'Sir Laurence inveigled himself in a foolish plea which occasioned his attendance for 30 sessions before the Lords of Session.' The reason was to gain legal complusion for the said eldest son, Patrick, then aged 22, to marry a sister of the Marquis of Douglas, supposed to be aged about 45, this bargain having been made up without his son so much as seeing the lady. Patrick cut short the legalities, however, by going off and secretly marrying Margaret Murray, daughter of the minister of Trinity Gask. Patrick was thereupon disinherited from the main estates of Gask, which were given to his younger brother Laurence, and the small place of Williamstoun settled on the independent heir, and this house built, about 1657.

Later, of course, the Oliphants of Gask were famous Jacobites, and when Prince Charles Edward breakfasted at Gask House on 11th September 1745, no doubt some of his lieutenants would lodge at Williamstoun nearby—the laird being then an A.D.C. to the Prince. Gask in consequence was severely harried by the Hanoverians the following February—but history is silent as to whether Williamstoun suffered the same fate.

STIRLINGSHIRE

AIRTH CASTLE

This is a most interesting, attractive and well preserved house. Standing high above Airth village, looking out over the plain of the Forth, it is a composite structure of at least four periods. The original castle has been a typical square freestanding tower, of probably the 15th century, now forming the south-west corner. It is four storeys and a garret in height, with a crenellated parapet without rounds at the angles. The next oldest portion is the south-east tower, a picturesque 16th-century structure, involved as to its upper works, which comprise a tall stair-turret with conical roof, another lesser two-storeyed turret corbelled out in the re-entrant, plus a platform roof within a parapet which is projected on corbelling only at the east side and which has one open round. Add to this the unusual chimney arrangements, and you have a complicated but highly attractive composition. Linking these two towers is a substantial main block of approximately the same height, with four dormer windows, dating probably from the late 16th or early 17th centuries; another wing stretched northwards from the east tower, possibly of the same period. This ends in a vast chimney-stack for the wide kitchen fireplace in the basement. A sham castellated front, in the English tradition, was added in the early 19th century, to the north.

The original building is called Wallace's tower, but does not date from so early a period. There was however a castle on the site at that time, for Blind Harry tells how Wallace sacked it when it was held by 100 Englishmen, to release his uncle, the priest of Dunipace, held prisoner within.

Internally there has been much alteration to link with various stages of building. The ground floor is vaulted. Built in over a doorway of the east tower, formerly external, is the motto

LAT THEM SAY, dated 1581. Many windows have been enlarged.

Edward, second son of Sir Robert Bruce of Clackmannan married Agnes, the heiress of the Airths or Erths of that Ilk in the 15th century, and obtained the property. He may have built the west tower. The castle was burned by James Third in 1488, before the fatal Battle of Sauchieburn, the next laird having joined the rebel lords supporting Prince James against his father. He received £100 next year, in compensation, from the new King James Fourth, 'for byggen of his Place that was brynt'. His grandson Sir Alexander married the Earl of Linlithgow's daughter in 1547. He it would be who built the east tower. A Bruce heiress carried Airth to the Elphinstones of nearby Elphinstone Tower, formerly called Airthbeg, three generations later. Her son Charles was killed in a duel with his relative, William Bruce of Auchenbowie nearby. Judge Graham acquired Airth in 1717, and it remained with that family until comparatively recent times.

The Earldom of Airth conferred, for peculiar reasons, on William Graham, 7th Earl of Menteith, seems to have had no connection with Airth Castle.

AUCHENBOWIE HOUSE

This handsome and commodious mansion belongs to the very end of the defensive period, in aspect. But although it appears to date substantially from the second half of the 17th century, there is much older work incorporated. A renewed heraldic panel is inserted over the original entrance in the foot of the stair-tower, bearing the Bruce arms and the date 1506. The walls at the southern end of the house are very thick, and this undoubtedly is the nucleus of the original fortalice.

There have been large additions to the west and north, but the house as it was in the 17th century has been an L-planned building of three storeys and an attic, with a semi-hexagonal stair-tower in the re-entrant angle, the walling being harled and yellow-washed. There are no defensive features remaining.

At an early date the lands belonged to the Cunninghams of Polmaise Cunningham nearby, but were bought by Robert Bruce who was Provost of Stirling in 1555. He it was who probably built the earlier portions of the existing house. A later laird, Captain William Bruce, killed a relative, Charles Elphinstone of Airth Castle, in a duel at the end of the 17th century, and he it may have been who enlarged the house in the first instance. In 1708 the Bruce heiress carried the property to Major-General George Munro, and their descendants are still in possession.

AUCHENVOLE CASTLE

Although Auchenvole is actually situated in that detached portion of Dunbartonshire that is surrounded by Stirlingshire, since it is now considered part of the burgh of Kilsyth in the latter country, it is convenient to deal with it here.

The house, situated on the south bank of the Kelvin, appears to date from the late 16th or early 17th century, with large modern additions. The original building is rather unusual, an L-planned structure with a very tiny stair-turret above third-floor level leading to a small watch-chamber in a gabled raising of the main block. There is one angle-turret on the north-west corner, but otherwise the walls are plain. There has been considerable alteration, especially to the south-west, where the additions have been erected.

The ground floor is vaulted, with a wide arched kitchen fireplace in one gable. A fairly wide turnpike stair rises to second-floor level. The building, though still occupied, is unfortunately not in a very good state, the clutter of outhouses detracting from the appearance.

Auchenvole, or Auchinvoil, seems to have been built by the family of Stark, under the superiority of the Lords Fleming of Cumbernauld, Earls of Wigton. James Stark was served heir of Thomas Stark of Auchenvoil in 1643.

The castle is said to be haunted by a lady who sat at a high window night after night, looking over at a clump of trees near the Kelvin where her lover, treacherously slain, was buried.

BARDOWIE CASTLE

Pleasantly situated on the north shore of Bardowie Loch about two miles east of Milngavie, at the very south-western corner of the county, this is a well-preserved castle of probably early 16th-century construction, altered in its upper works later in the same century, to which a more modern mansion has been attached. There are one or two especially interesting features.

The building, oblong on plan, would appear to have been originally a typical parapeted free-standing tower, with garret storey within the parapet-walk. But in a reconstruction, the upper storey was altered to house something like a second Hall, the gables being brought flush with the end walls, with the roof oversailing the parapet-walk to rest on the parapet itself. Thus, the three small garret-storey windows seen in the sketch are probably only enlargements of the crenellations of the original parapet. This is above the lateral wallheads only; whether there were parapets to crown the end walls is not now ascertainable. At the sides, however, the original walks are still there, under the eaves of the roof, forming narrow corridors.

Within this rebuilt upper storey, the gallery or Hall has a very fine open timber roof—something very rare in Scotland. It consists of massive but graceful rafters and ties constructed to give something of an impression of ribbed stone vaulting. Whoever effected this alteration went to a lot of trouble to do so.

The entrance to the castle was by a round-headed doorway in the south front, which gives access to the vaulted basement and to a straight stair in the thickness of the walling, leading to the Hall on the first floor. Another straight mural stair ascends to the second floor, this being now the final storey. Small stairs at diagonally opposite ends of this fine apartment, one a turnpike at the north-west corner and the other straight, in the thickness of the south-east walling, lead up higher to the covered parapet-walks at either side, which do not connect—a thoroughly unusual arrangement.

The reason for all this quite elaborate re-arrangement which resulted in, whatever else, a major curtailing of domestic and bedroom space, would be interesting to know.

Bardowie was at an early date a seat of the family of Galbraith, once powerful in this area, also settled at Culcreuch, Craigmaddie and Gartconnel Castles comparatively nearby. Their line ended in the 14th century in an heiress, married to a Keith, whose daughter Janet, in turn, carried the properties to David Hamilton of Cadzow, ancestor of the Dukes of Hamilton. The Stirlings of Keir appear to have had a connection with Bardowie in the 16th century, but just what this was is not entirely clear; possibly it was only the superiority. It seems at anyrate that it was the Hamiltons who built the present castle. A junior branch of this family retained possession for many generations, and keep cropping up in Scottish history, in national affairs and local feuds, seemingly not being noted for their peaceable dispositions. John was killed in a quarrel with the Logans of Balvie in 1526, not far from Bardowie. His son and successor Allan, likewise died in a struggle, with Campbells. In 1591 another laird of Bardowie, William, was involved in a serious quarrel with Graham of nearby Dougalston. And so on. It would seem likely that these three were those involved in the construction and alteration of the castle as we now see it. The last, and sixteenth of the line, was Robert Hamilton, who was succeeded by his sister, married to Thomas Buchanan of Spittal and Leny, which family thereupon incorporated Hamilton into their name.

In 1707, Mary, sister of John Hamilton of Bardowie, married the gallant Gregor Black Knee MacGregor of Glengyle, Rob Roy's nephew and chieftain.

CASTLECARY

This interesting and fairly well preserved tower, dating probably from the late 15th or early 16th century, stands above the Red Burn, which here forms the boundary between the counties of Stirling and Dunbarton, some seven miles west of Falkirk. Its site has always been one of strategic importance, being plumb on one of the most vital routes of communication in Scotland; here was one of the principal stations on Antoninus's Roman Wall, and here today, at a short distance, run two main railway lines, the road, and the Forth and Clyde Canal.

The building is oblong on plan, measuring 34 by 23 feet, the tower rising 42 feet to the parapet. The walls are of rubble with worked stone dressings. The original entrance is at the west end of the north front, and gives access to the stair-foot, a turnpike, the well of which projects somewhat into the north-west corner of each chamber—a rather clumsy arrangement which builders of a later period were apt to get over by adding an outwards-projecting stair-tower or wing. The stair has uneven steps, and rises to the parapet where it finishes in a plain caphouse, unusual in having a lean-to roof. Also unusual is the way in which the garret storey above is entered from this caphouse, at parapet-level.

The ground floor is vaulted, with the Hall on first floor and the usual private accommodation above. The parapet-walk, which is not provided with open rounds at the angles, is well-drained by numerous cannon-like spouts. At parapet-level at the east end of the north front is a small machicolated projection, for the purpose of dropping down missiles, molten metal, or boiling water on unwelcome guests. Why it should have been placed here, and not above the doorway as is normal, is something of a mystery. On the centre section of the crenellated parapet on the south front is carved a small heraldic shield and face, but all features of both are now obliterated.

There is a lower addition to the tower on the east side, dating from 1679. This is now only two storeys in height, but has been a storey higher. It is L-shaped on plan, the small wing at the north-west corner housing another turnpike stair.

The interior has been modernised, and the castle is still occupied.

There was formerly a courtyard to the north, and there is a fine old walled garden to the south. A good specimen of iron yett or grille is still preserved within, part of the original door defence.

The Baillie family were long resident here, and it was presumably the birthplace of Alexander Baillie the famous antiquary. The story is told of how his sister Lizzie leapt from one of the windows into the plaid of one Donald Graham, a handsome young Highland farmer whom she had met on the island of Inchmahome. Laird Baillie was much against his richly-dowered daughter wasting herself upon any poor Highlandman, and the result was this elopement and the following verse.

> 'Shame light on the loggerheads,
> that live at Castlecary,
> To let awa' the bonnie lass
> the Highlandman to marry.'

The property later passed to that branch of the great family of Dundas which became Earls and Marquises of Zetland.

The castle was burned by a party of Highlanders during the Rising of 1715.

CULCREUCH

Standing in a large estate on the southern slopes of the Fintry Hills, a mile from Fintry village, this is a handsome fortalice of probably late 15th-century origin, which has been added to in the early 18th century. The early building is a fairly typical tower, oblong on plan, constructed of good coursed rubble, rising through three main storeys to a crenellated parapet, which may have been renewed, borne on fairly elaborate chequered corbelling, with a garret storey above. There are no rounds at the angles. The walk is remarkable for the large number of its drainage spouts.

The entrance, now covered by the later work, was in the east wall, and gave access to the vaulted basement and the stairway. The usual arrangement of Hall on first floor and bedrooms above would apply. The windows of the old tower have been somewhat enlarged at the time of the 18th-century extension. Recently the vent of a garderobe, for sanitation, has been traced in the thickness of the west wall. A partly obliterated carving, probably heraldic, appears over the present doorway in the addition, only the date 1721 and the initials M.L. surviving.

Culcreuch was a property of the Galbraith and Napier families, passing eventually to an enterprising proprietor, Alexander Spiers, who about 1796 erected a large cotton-mill on the estate, giving much employment. The heiress married Sir George Home, tenth baronet of Blackadder, in the mid-19th century, who took the name of Home-Spiers.

The old house is in good order, and still occupied.

ELPHINSTONE TOWER

All that remains of the ancient fortalice and seat of the well-known family of Elphinstone, that played so large a part in Scottish history. Standing on a rocky bluff above the flat lands of the Carse of Forth, it soars over the surrounding trees of Dunmore Park—as the property was later called.

It is a simple square tower, probably of late 15th-century date, rising four storeys to a parapet that has open rounds at all angles save the south-west, where a stair-turret of later appearance rises from third-storey level, to end in a conical-roofed caphouse. There would probably be the usual gabled garret storey within the parapet, but this has now gone. The marks of additional building can be seen against the west walling.

The tower has suffered considerable alteration at various periods, and the parapet seems to have been renewed, as has the stair-turret. Most of the windows have been altered and 'romantic-ised'. The round-headed door is in the south front, with the stairway rising to the left.

The lands, earlier known as Airthbeg, and adjoining Airth Castle, came to John Elphinstone from East Lothian by marriage with Marjory the heiress before 1340. The present tower was probably built by Sir John, the 'King's familiar shield-bearer', father of the first Lord Elphinstone, who died in 1508. His son was killed at Flodden, with the King. In 1784, the eleventh lord sold the property to the Earl of Dunmore, who once again changed the name.

DUCHRAY CASTLE

Remotely situated amid picturesque wooded country a mile to the south of Loch Ard and about·three miles from Aberfoyle, Duchray is a delightful small fortalice which has been much altered in its upper storeys and windows. It appears to date substantially from the late 16th century, but almost certainly older work is incorporated in its lower storeys. It consists of an oblong main block of three storeys and a garret, with a large circular stair-tower rising at the south-east angle, and a corner-turret crowning the opposite north-west angle. Both these have been somewhat reduced in height, unfortunately. The massive walls are of good coursed rubble, but the windows have been 'gothicised' and somewhat enlarged. One of the original windows, now built up, may still be traced, however, high on the east gable. Additional building has been extended to north-east and to west, to enclose a courtyard. The ground to the north has been somewhat levelled and built up. The site formerly would be a strong one, on the edge of a burn's ravine.

The entrance is in the usual place at the foot òf the stair-tower. The basement is vaulted, and now forms a delightful sitting-room. Originally, no doubt, it contained the kitchen. The Hall was on the first floor, with a private room to the east, and above are bedrooms, that to the west having the angle-turret opening off.

This fortalice was a strength of the great family of Graham for long, but in 1528 the lands of Duchray were occupied by George Buchanan of that Ilk, under the superiority of Queen Margaret, widow of James Fourth, as liferentrix of the Stewardry of Menteith. In 1569 Duchray was sold, however, to John Graham of Downance, cadet of the Graham Earls of Menteith. The castle substantially therefore would be built by either John Graham or his son William, possibly on the foundations of an earlier building. Its massive walls would be highly necessary against the depredations of the neighbouring warlike clan of MacGregor, seldom friends of the Grahams. Nevertheless, tradition says that it gave good shelter on at least one occasion to the famous freebooter Rob Roy MacGregor himself. He was visiting the place, for purposes unspecified, when a contingent of Redcoats searching for him arrived. The two Graham sisters in residence played excellent hosts, however. While one, considered to be somewhat simple, kept the officers engaged in talk, the other got Rob smuggled out by a side door, the position of which, though built-up, is still to be seen, and down into the burn's ravine.

On an earlier occasion Duchray Castle was the headquarters of the Earl of Glencairn's expedition in 1653 in favour of King Charles Second, the only real attempt made in Scotland to throw off the Protector Cromwell's nine years rule of the country. Though this attempt was unsuccessful, the battle with Monck's forces in the Pass of Aberfoyle was a victory, and in this both Graham of Duchray with his troop of foot, and the neighbouring MacGregors, took a vigorous part. Graham continued to assist Glencairn, in the King's cause, and suffered much therefor. Charles does not seem to have been as grateful as he might have been, for it was not until the accession of James Seventh and Second that the Scottish Treasury was authorised to pay the Laird of Duchray One Hundred Pounds sterling in consideration of his loyalty and losses.

Duchray Castle is said to have been burned after the Jacobite Rising of the Forty-five, which accounts for the altered upper storey. The house is still occupied, although no longer owned by the Grahams, and appreciatively cared for.

DUNTREATH CASTLE

This formerly large and important castle has undergone many changes of fortune in its long history, and to chronicle the stages of its growth and subsequent diminishments would require much space. What now remains is the original keep, somewhat altered, and a modernised portion of later work. Much else has been demolished in fairly recent years. The entire castle was abandoned at about 1740 and stood a ruin until the mid-19th century.

Although probably originally consisting of this keep of possibly early 15th-century construction, the establishment grew into a large courtyard-type castle, within curtain walling 120 feet long by 100 broad, with secondary buildings, including an especially fine gatehouse tower, another known as the Dumb Laird's Tower, and a chapel. These were mainly 17th-century additions.

The keep, oblong on plan, stood at the north-west corner of the courtyard. It is a massive building, three main storeys and a garret in height, of unusual design in that it is a double tower, each floor containing two chambers divided by a thick partition wall. The crenellated parapet is borne on individual corbelling, and the roof above has been renewed.

An interesting feature is the porch-like arrangement for the original entrance (the door seen in sketch is a later modification). This built-out porch continues upwards, appearing not so much a tower as a buttress, diminishing and being backset as it rises, to end in a round caphouse at parapet-level, which however is modern. Partly contained within this buttresslike tower is the turnpike stair—a most unusual arrangement.

There has inevitably been considerable alteration to the building, within and without. The machicolated projections seen in sketch could have been used as outfalls for garderobes rather than for defence.

Duntreath came to a younger branch of the Edmonstone family, in the person of Sir William of Culloden, who had married the Princess Mary, daughter of Robert Third, on the forfeiture of the last Celtic Earl of Lennox in 1425. It has remained with this family ever since. In 1578, Sir James Edmonstone, 6th of Duntreath, had a grant from the Earl of Argyll, Justice-General of Scotland, for holding courts at this fortalice. One of the 17th-century lairds was born dumb, but seems otherwise to have been quite effective, and built the afore-mentioned tower. After his death the family removed to live on estates it had acquired in Ireland, for nearly a century, and Duntreath was allowed to fall into ruin. It may have been at this time that the chapel, during the celebration of divine service, is said to 'have undergone a crash'. The Edmonstones returned to Scotland in 1783, and lived at Colzium, near Kilsyth, not far away, until 1863 when Duntreath was restored and they returned to their original seat.

The remaining portions of the castle are still occupied by the present baronet and family. It stands on the right bank of the Blane water, in a fine estate, about three miles north-west of Strathblane and ten north of Glasgow.

The Edmonstones are thought to have originally been a branch of the powerful East Scotland house of Seton, and in 1248 and earlier were settled on lands of that name in Midlothian.

KERSIE

This is a pleasant, modest laird's house, now a farmhouse but in excellent condition, mainly dating from the 17th century, but with a nucleus of probably 16th century work. It stands near the south bank of Forth almost opposite Alloa, four miles north of Airth. It appears as a mansion with park, in Pont's Map of 1654.

Kersie is an L-shaped building of three storeys and a garret, with a squared wide stair-tower in the re-entrant, the walls being harled and the gables plain. Undoubtedly the south-west corner contains the remains of an earlier house, probably a free-standing small tower. On the angle of this wall, at second-floor level, is a two-faced sundial. A feature of the house is the moulded surrounds of all windows, unusual at this late period. An outside short stairway in the centre of the south front admits to a door formed out of a first floor window, a late 17th-century alteration, as at Pilrig, Edinburgh, and Pilmuir, East Lothian. The original doorway, notably off the straight, is in the foot of the stair-tower.

Internally the house has been much altered and modernised, but there are two good moulded fireplaces. In the now semi-subterranean basement, at the oldest corner, there has been a wide arched kitchen fireplace, built up, with a wall-cupboard adjoining in which is a filled-in gunloop. There is an arrow-slit window nearby.

Kersie is thought to have been built by a branch of the ancient family of Menteith of West Kerse.

LITTLE SAUCHIE (or SAUCHIEBURN) CASTLE

Remote from main roads, within the large estate of Sauchieburn, three miles from Stirling, this partly ruined fortalice, probably of the late 16th century, stands in a strong position. It is an L-shaped building with a later, probably 17th-century extension, now used as the estate-office.

The original has been a picturesque house of four storeys, with angle-turrets on the northern corners and a stair-turret above first floor level on the east front. Nearby rises a tall narrow gablet, which has enclosed a watch-chamber. The walls are well provided with splayed gunloops and circular shot-holes.

The basement contains two vaulted chambers, and a wide squared stair rises from the entrance in the re-entrant, to the first floor. Here was the Hall, a fine apartment lit with six large windows and one small. The turnpike stair in the turret rises to the second storey, now floorless, containing two apartments, with another in the wing above the squared stairway. The inward projection of the corner-turrets' corbelling is unusual. Above were attics and the watch-chamber.

The extension contains a large unvaulted kitchen with arched fireplace, the massive chimney for which is prominent. Above is a handsome room with coved ceiling, now the office.

The fortalice was probably built by James Erskine, half-brother of John, Lord Erskine, after 1541. In the 18th century the property came to the Ramsay family, with whose descendants it remains. The Battle of Sauchieburn was fought nearby.

GARGUNNOCK HOUSE

On a pleasant shelf of the foothills overlooking the former level mosses of the Forth some five miles west of Stirling, and just to the east of the village of the same name, stands the composite and interesting mansion of Gargunnock. It is a very ancient name in Scotland's story, for Sir William Wallace is said to have taken up a position on Keir Hill, approximately where the mansion now stands, while an English garrison held the Peel of Gargunnock, an earlier fortalice on the low ground near the fords of the river—from which he presently drove the invaders, and which he garrisoned himself. Of this castle no trace now remains.

The present house dates from various periods, but the discernible nucleus appears to have been an L-shaped structure of the late 16th century, although still older work may well be incorporated. The wing of this early house still projects boldly to the east, crowned by a single angle-turret and rather unusually shaped crowstepped gable. Its main block, running north and south, still forms the central axis of the mansion, although there have been large additions at both ends in the 17th century and later. It is reputed to have had, previous to 1790, a high wall and strong gate in front, and also a moat, so that obviously it was a place of strength; but of these no traces remain.

The early house is three storeys and an attic in height; the walls, in some places being four feet in thickness, are roughcast. Probably there have been more angle-turrets than the one remaining, for inevitably there has been drastic reconstruction throughout. The original door has been in the re-entrant angle, facing south, but this has been built-up and harled over. The door in the east front is modern. The ground floor is vaulted, and has been subdivided at a later date. There is a filled-in gunloop in the west wall at basement level at the south end, and the wide arch of the kitchen fireplace can be traced, with certain recesses in the thickness of the masonry. The turnpike stairway has formerly risen in the re-entrant angle, near the doorway, but has been replaced. The Hall on the first floor has been altered also, but there is a delightful room at this level in the wing, still with its white-painted pine panelling. The house is in excellent condition.

There are records of a house here in 1460 when Alexander

Seton was served heir of his mother, heiress of the Normavils. It is possible that he built the earliest work incorporated in this site. By 1513 however, Ninian Seton pays entry money for a sixth part of Gargunnock 'with the tower, fortalice and mansion of the same', so that it was presumably this laird or his successor who built the L-shaped house described. There may be a certain amount of confusion with regard to the history of Gargunnock proper and the nearby fortalice of Touch to the east, which at one time seems to have been incorporated in the Gargunnock barony. There were, of course, Seton lairds at Touch. By 1740, Colonel Campbell of Ardkinglass, Governor of Stirling Castle and an anti-Jacobite, appears as proprietor—so that there may well have been interesting doings here during the period a few years later when Prince Charles Edward's star was in the ascendant. The ancient sundial in the garden is said to bear the Colonel's name and arms. The estate was purchased by John Stirling, of that important local family, at the end of the 18th century, and happily still remains in the possession of his descendants.

OLD LECKIE HOUSE

Picturesquely situated on the wooded lower slopes of the hills south of the wide Carse of Stirling, six miles west of the town, Old Leckie is an attractive laird's house of probably late 16th-century date, now superceded by a modern mansion, but still occupied by estate employees. It conforms to the T-plan, with a main block of three storeys and a four-storey wing projecting in the centre. A stair-turret is corbelled out above first floor level in the north-west re-entrant, and beneath it is set a shallow archway recessed within which is the original entrance, still complete with its stout iron yett, and beside it a tiny guard window, also with grille, and a shot-hole below—the whole forming an interesting composition. Above is an empty panel-space, from which it is said the Moir crest has been removed—in which case the panel would be a late 17th century addition. The walls are harled and the gables crowstepped in the usual manner.

Internally the house has been much altered, both at an early date and later, to form a tenement for workers. Part of the ground floor is vaulted, and part not—which seems to suggest that a still older building is incorporated. The entrance admits to a passage serving the basement chambers, and also to a narrow turnpike stair projecting slightly in the opposite re-entrant angle of the T, which rises only to the first floor. This is another unusual feature, the normal arrangement for such a plan being for a wide stair to occupy all or most of the base of the wing as far as the first floor, before the ascent is continued in the narrower turret-stair. This present tiny stairway as the only access to the Hall and main living quarters on the first floor must have been very inconvenient, and it is small wonder that, in more settled days, the handsome outside stone staircase was added to the north of the wing.

A Mordaco de Leckie held the lands in 1406, which indicates a house on the site then. But the property seems to have fallen to the Crown, no doubt through the laird taking the wrong side in one of the innumerable dynastic struggles of the time, for King James Second conveys it in 1451 to Adam Cosure, a burgess of Stirling for 'faithful services rendered'. These services were in fact the loan of 300 merks to the King, for Cosure was a moneylender. Cosure did not wish to give up the property apparently, when James Third tried to repay his father's debt

21 years later, and there were court proceedings, of all places before the high altar of the parish church at Stirling, where Cosure adopted an obstinate and Shylock-like attitude. But it seems that King and nobility would not countenance such a character as a Scots laird, and the necessary pressure was presumably brought to bear, for, four days after, William Lord Monypenny—a name which might more aptly fit the other—was infeft in Leckie by no less than a precept from Chancery. Amusingly enough, Monypenny, a friend of the King, sold the lands only two months later to Andrew, Lord Avondale.

In the next century, however, John Leckie of Leckie, apparently a descendant of the original family, who had retained possession of adjoining property, repurchased the lands. He, or his son, probably built the present house, for he had the whole estate erected into the Barony of Leckie in 1535. About 1659 Bailie David Moir, of Stirling, acquired the lands from the Leckies, and the descendants of this family retained possession until earlier this century.

MUGDOCK CASTLE

What remains here, unfortunately, is only a small part of what has been one of the most interesting castles in Scotland, the early seat of the great Graham of Montrose family, and the home of the famous Marquis. Sad to say, even such remains as there are, are in a bad state of neglect.

The castle stands, some distance from any road, in somewhat hilly ground in the parish of Strathblane, about seven miles north of Glasgow. Its position is a strong one, the ground falling away abruptly on two sides, and with Mugdock Loch, formerly much larger than now, guarding it on the west. The original castle has been a very large one, within a curiously long and narrow courtyard area, fully 320 feet in length. The remaining entire tower, seen in sketch, has formed only the south-west corner of the whole; whether this was in fact the main keep, or only one of the flanking towers, is not now possible to say. The vaulted basement of another tower remains some distance to the north, and since this seems to have been approximately of the same size, it may be that there was a larger keep elsewhere. The ruins of a chapel are traceable away at the north-east end of the enclosure. A large modern mansion in the Scottish Baronial style was built in the central area of the enclosure last century, and though this is now a complete ruin, it hides the traces of previous work. A 16th and 17th-century range of buildings has been added to the west, outside the original curtain walling.

The remaining tower is square on plan, tall and somewhat slender in aspect, rising through four storeys to its parapet, 60 feet above the ground. There is a garret storey above, though this has been renewed. The parapet is not crenellated, and rises flush with the walling. Interesting is the way the upper walling above second-floor level has been built out, on single individual corbels on the south front and on a continuing tapering course on the west. The reason seems to have been to give added space in the thickness of the walling for a straight stair to the parapet and for mural chambers. The quality of the masonry is very good.

The basement, entered from the courtyard, has no connection with the upper floors, but up a few steps is a very complete garderobe in the thickness of the walling—a peculiar arrangement for what would seem to have been merely a storage room.

Possibly the chamber was used as some sort of guardroom for the portcullis gateway nearby on the south, now gone.

The tower's main entrance is at first floor, reached by an outside stone stair. It has a ribbed vaulted ceiling. A turnpike stair rises in the thickness of the south-east angle—though the walling of the exterior is very slightly built out to receive it. The second floor is on the level of the extremely high curtain walling of the courtyard.

The later building to the west, outside the courtyard, apparently largely dates from 1655.

This ancient barony was acquired from Maldwin, Earl of Lennox in the 13th century by David de Graham, from whom descended the Montrose family. Certainly none of the remaining work is as old as that. The castle suffered many vicissitudes in its long history. When the Marquis was a prisoner in Edinburgh Castle in 1641, the Lord Sinclair demolished 'his staitly house of Mugdock', but only superficially presumably, for Montrose was living here again before his famous campaign of 1644. Part of the castle was allowed to fall into ruin after being harried by the Buchanans in that year.

PLEAN CASTLE

Standing in open country a mile east of Plean village, this is a small plain tower of possibly 15th-century construction with later alterations. Its position would be strong, standing on a rocky mound surrounded by marshland. Though a ruin, it was restored after a fashion in recent times, but is once more roofless, though the walls are sound. Unfortunately the modern upper storey above parapet-level is unsightly.

The original walls rise three storeys to the parapet corbelling, above which would be the usual garret within gables. There have been open rounds at all corners save the north-east, where formerly would be the caphouse at the head of the stair which rises in this angle.

The present entrance in the south front is not original, nor is the inscription above it. The ground floor is not vaulted, strangely although the outbuildings of the courtyard are. A straight stair leads to the first floor, which was occupied by the Hall. This has a window with stone seats, two garderobes and a large fireplace. A turnpike stair rises to the second floor which has been sub-divided with two fireplaces, one large.

Remains of the courtyard building suggest a 16th-century construction. In one is a gunloop.

Plane, as it was formerly called, came by marriage with the heiress to a son of Lord Somerville in 1449, who probably built the present tower. It remained with that family for two centuries, when it passed to the Nicolsons of nearby Carnock.

Situated on the level flood-plain of the Forth three miles east of Stirling, and formerly called Wester Polmaise, this unusual little fortalice would occupy a strong position in the days before the land was drained. The building consists of a tall square whitewashed tower of four storeys, dating probably from the early 17th century, with a commodious wing of lesser height to the east, of possibly a century later.

The tower has a semi-circular stair-turret rising at the south-east angle, ending with the main roof oversailing it and a finishing of crowsteps—an unusual treatment which is probably a later alteration, and similar to that at Blairlogie across the Forth. The addition hides the base of this turret. The old entrance was in the west front, now built up. Inserted within this doorway is a heraldic panel with the motto GANG FORWARD and the initials A.S. and A.H.

The arms are those of the Stirling family, impaled probably with Hamilton, and seem to refer to Sir Alexander Stirling of Garden, a judge, who succeeded to Wester Polmaise on the death of his sister, widow of Alexander Cowan, a surgeon of Stirling who had bought it from the Murrays of Touchadam in the early 17th century. In this house is thought to have been detained the ill-fated Lady Grange, by her husband, another judge, before her enforced captivity and death in the Hebrides, in 1732.

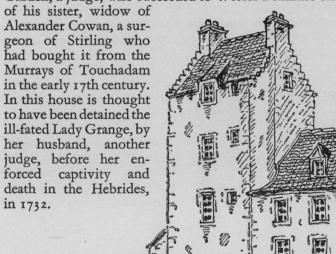

STENHOUSE

Situated on high ground above the loch that lies behind the great Carron Ironworks, and adjoining the modern township of Stenhousemuir in the Falkirk area, this is a handsome and commodious example of a prosperous laird's house of the early 17th century, that has been badly neglected in recent years. It was originally a tall house on the L-plan, with corner-turrets at the angles, that to the south-east being unusual in that it is square and not circular. A slight projection within the re-entrant angle indicates the position of the original stairway. Many of the windows have undoubtedly been enlarged when the large new extension was added in more modern times. This extension takes the form of a fairly exact replica of the early L-shaped house, projecting as another L to the west and north, to form a total plan approximating to the letter E, the central portion being partly filled in with a classical type balustraded porch and entrance hall.

The original house is four storeys and an attic in height, the ground floor being semi-subterranean. Unfortunately most of the attic dormers have lost their carved pediments, but one of these is built into the walling under the south-west angle-turret, and is dated 1622 with the initials w.b. and a.t. The south front has been much altered, windows having been filled in, and a modern doorway opened at first-floor level, with an outside staircase leading up to it.

There are various heraldic panels let into the walling, one on the north front bearing the arms of Bruce impaled with Douglas and dated 1655, with the initials s.w.b. and d.h.d. This was the second baronet, Sir William Bruce who married Helen, daughter of Douglas of Cavers. Another panel, more finely fashioned, is inset in the east wall, dated 1710 and adding to the heraldry the motto DO WELL AND DOUBT NOT.

Internally the building has been much altered, adapted and subdivided. On the ceiling of what was presumably once the Hall, on the first floor, now a vestibule, is a plaster heraldic ornament dated 1698.

The Bruces of Stenhouse stemmed from Sir William Bruce, second son of Sir Alexander Bruce of Airth, in the same county, who built this house. He had married the daughter of the 5th

Lord Fleming, whose aunt, therefore, would be one of Mary Queen of Scots' famed Marys. His grandson, also William, obtained a Nova Scotia baronetcy in 1628 with remainder to heirs male whatsoever. It was his son, a third Sir William, who married Douglas of Cavers' daughter. The next laird still, another Sir William, was 'out' in the Risings of 1715 and 1719. From his fourth son are descended the Comptes de Bruce of Paris. A grandson was 'out' again in the Forty-five. Two generations later, Sir Michael Bruce of Stenhouse was said to be the cause of the curse on the Bruce family, through removing stones from a much revered local landmark called Arthur's Oon, to build a dam. Certainly the family fortunes have much declined since he died in 1795.

Unfortunately this most attractive and interesting house has been allowed to fall into a bad state of repair. It has been the property of the great Carron Company for many years, and it is most regrettable that it should have come to its present neglected state, so as to be threatened even with demolition.

TOUCH HOUSE

On a fine estate in the lap of the Gargunnock Hills about three miles west of Stirling, stands this tall tower of probably 15th-century date, to which has been added a large mansion of the late 16th or early 17th century, and a later handsome classical frontage.

The original keep, which stands at the edge of a declivity, is practically square on plan, rising four storeys to the crenellated parapet, which however returns round only the south and east sides, though it is probable that it formerly girded the entire tower. There are no rounds at the angles. A gabled garret storey rises within the parapet.

A most intriguing feature is the manner in which the north-east corner, though now filled in to the square with masonry, has formerly been cut away in an L-shaped cavity from top to bottom. The original faced bonding stones on both fronts are perfectly clear, showing that the early tower was designed this way. The reason for this is not clear. The stairway rises in the angle nearby, and may have been widened when the cavity was filled in—for it is a wide stair for a tower of this age; but this does not explain the reason for the gap in the first place. I have never seen another keep thus built.

The original doorway, now built over, no doubt lay near the foot of the stairway. The tower is now entered from the later work. The ground floor is vaulted, and there is a chamber on each floor, each having a garderobe or closet in the thickness of the east wall. The stairway ends in a curious little cap-house with a steep lean-to roof at parapet-level, to which it admits.

The range of later work to the north is commodious and substantial, but plain, with steep roofs, dormer windows and crow-stepped gables but no turrets or other ornament. In contrast, the south facade, which forms the present front of the mansion, is very fine, crowned with a large heraldic tympanum.

The property was in early times known as Touch Fraser, and in 1234 Bernard Fraser thereof was appointed to the hereditary office of Sheriff of Stirlingshire. A Sir Richard Fraser, from the county of Stirling, did homage to Edward of England at Berwick in 1296, on the Ragman Roll. Touch Fraser was regranted by Robert the Bruce to Alexander Fraser thereafter. By 1510 however we read that King James Fourth 'for his special affection' infefts anew Alexander Seton of Tulchfrasere in the barony of the same 'which the said Alexander and his predecessors have enjoyed for so longpast'. Nevertheless, in 1426 John Stewart, Earl of Buchan was in possession, being at that time himself hereditary Sheriff of Stirlingshire, and he it may well have been who built the tower we see today. How it came to him, and what happened to the Frasers, is not clear. However, the Seton family thereafter seem to have retained possession for a very long period, and it would be they who added the various extensions.

In 1708, the laird of Touch was one of five lairds involved in an abortive attempt to place the Old Pretender on the throne, a venture in which Rob Roy was implicated. These five were arrested, sent to London, but later returned to Edinburgh for trial. They escaped sentence through mishandling of the trial by the Lord Advocate.

It is good that, after a period during the late war and afterwards as a hospital, Touch House is once again inhabited as a house, and in the possession of a branch of the ancient family of Buchanan that had a previous connection with it.

MUCH-ALTERED STRUCTURES

A LIST, by no means exhaustive, of fortified houses which, although dating in some part from the defensive period, and surviving, have been so altered at a later period as to leave little of the earlier work visible, or to offer a wholly different appearance.

FIFE
Balcarres House
Comrie Castle
Culross Abbey House

PERTHSHIRE
Balhousie Castle
The Coldoch
Gartincaber
Keir House
Kilbryde Castle
Lanrick Castle

Leny House
Logie-almond
Rednock House
Rossie Ochil
Strathallan Castle

STIRLINGSHIRE
Bannockburn House
Callander House, Falkirk
Muiravonside House
Skaithmuir Tower

CREICH CASTLE

Little known, Creich is in fact in no very difficult or remote situation, on the fairly high ground in the North of Fife, less than 2 miles north of the village of Luthrie and a similar distance south of the Firth of Tay, on the farm of the same name. Indeed the farmhouse stands close by. Nevertheless there is a feeling of remoteness about the vicinity and wooded hillsides.

The castle appears to date from the late 16th century, although there must have been earlier work on the defensive site, for Creich was a possession of a branch of the well-known Fife family of Beaton or Bethune, and in the earlier part of that century Elizabeth Beaton of Creich was a mistress of James the Fifth and cousin of Cardinal David Beaton. The building conforms to the usual L-plan, with a squared stair-tower in the re-entrant angle facing south-west. There have been three main storeys and a garret in the roof, although this has now gone; but the walling is fairly entire to eaves-level. A noteworthy feature is the quite elaborate decorative corbelling which supported and projected a caphouse or watch-chamber at the head of the stair-tower, and possibly an open bartizan or balcony adjoining on the west

wing. There have been angle-turrets on both wings, the corbelling for which still survives.

The doorway in the foot of the stair-tower is round-headed, with an arrow-slit type shot-hole above. The walling throughout is not very thick, which usually indicates a fairly late date, as does the chamfering of the window-surrounds. The interior is badly fallen in. The basement has been vaulted and the stair a turnpike.

There is a gabled dovecote some fifty yards to the north, probably once within a courtyard.

The original owners of Creich appear to have been a family called Liddall. In James the Third's reign Sir James Liddall was involved in a treasonable plot to put the then Duke of Albany on the throne; he was attainted and estates forfeited and thereafter the lands of Creich sold by his son to David Beaton, a younger son of John Beaton of Balfour, and therefore probably an uncle of the famous Cardinal Beaton. In 1586 the King confirmed James Beaton of Creich and his wife Margaret Wemyss, in the tower, fortalice and lands of Creich in the barony of Dunbog. He was then Keeper of the Palace of Falkland. Another James Beaton of Creich sat in the Scots Parliament in 1644-45.

DENMILN CASTLE, FIFE

Standing at the roadside, in a farm-steading, one mile south-east of Newburgh, this is a rather unusual fortalice of the late 16th century, ruinous but with the main features surviving. Its cruciform plan is almost unique, with a main block lying approximately east and west, a squared stair-wing projecting centrally to the north, and opposite this a peculiar smaller rectangular tower, solid stone at the foot but on each of the upper floors housing a tiny lobby. This is used to enable access to be gained round the end of the central partition wall which divides each storey of the main block into two apartments, without the need for an intercommunicating door therein — a highly unusual arrangement. It seems hardly conceivable that the builders should have gone to the trouble of erecting this special tower for this purpose, and it may have originally had some other function, perhaps to house garderobes. Even so, it is a strange feature.

The castle contains three main storeys, with a garret floor above. A parapet and walk crowned the east gable only, supported on masive individual corbels of three members, with cannon-like spouts for draining the walk still projecting above. The windows are fairly large, and there are a number of wide splayed gunloops at basement level. The moulded entrance is in the re-entrant angle facing north-west, in the foot of the stair-wing, guarded by gunloops. It opens on to the foot of a fairly wide turnpike. The basement contains two vaulted chambers, neither provided with the usual wide arched fireplace which represents the kitchen. Each of the upper rooms, two to each storey, has a fireplace; presumably the larger apartment at first-floor level was the Hall. There has been a courtyard to the west, and it seems probable that the kitchen premises were housed in a lean-to building therein. A dovecote to the south is dated 1706, with the initials of Sir Michael Balfour and his wife Dame Marjory Moncrieff.

In 1452 Denmylne was given to James Balfour, son of Sir John Balfour of Balgarvy, by James the Second for faithful service, and the family held the property until 1710. The burial aisle was in the old ruined St. Magridin's church at Abdie, near Lindores Loch, and memorials include one to Sir Michael, member of the royal household of Charles the Second who 'died of old age and disease 1652 in his 72nd year'; and his son Sir James, knight-baronet, Lord Lyon King of Arms, well-known antiquary and friend of Drummond of Hawthornden, a 'student of the distant past accurate as he was eager, the darling and apple of the eye of the Muses', died 1657. A brother of this last was Sir Andrew Balfour, 1630-94, physician and founder of Edinburgh's first botanical garden.

DOUNE CASTLE, PERTHSHIRE

This magnificent castle, one of the most famous in the land, was built at the end of the 14th and beginning of the 15th centuries, to succeed the stronghold on Inch Talla in the Lake of Menteith as the principle messuage-place of the great earldom of Menteith, or more properly Monteith. It stands in a strong site above the junction of the Ardoch Burn and the River Teith, just below the town of Doune. Although probably containing an older nucleus, most of the present building was erected by Robert, Duke of Albany — who married the Menteith heiress — and his son, Murdoch, both Regents during the long captivitiy of their kinsman James the First.

The castle consists of two great and tall keeps, linked by a lower range, to form the north side of a quadrangular courtyard, the other three sides being enclosed by a 40-foot-high curtain-wall, 8 feet thick, crowned by a parapet and walk, with open circular turrets at the angles and semi-circular bartisans corbelled out midway. Of the two keeps, that to the north-east is the larger and higher, a massive, roughly rectangular building of five main storeys and a garret, with a semi-circular tower projecting at the north-east angle. It is crowned by a flush parapet flanking a gabled roof to north and south only, the wall-walks of these connecting only by open flights of steps up and over the pitched roof at each end — a highly unusual arrangement. The stairhead rises to form a lofty look-out platform, reached from the eastern flight of steps. The north-west keep is somewhat lower, four storeys and a garret, but also having a flush parapet and gabled roof. There are a number of machicolated projections here, three grouped fairly close together, the largest above a built-up arched-headed postern gate to the west. The area between the two keeps is occupied by a long two-storeyed building. The courtyard is large and contains a deep draw-well.

The entrance is by an arched gateway in the main keep, admitting to a steeply-rising, cobbled and vaulted pend, with a vaulted porter's lodge and inner chamber to one side, and a guardroom and dark bee-hive-vaulted pit or prison to the other. Elsewhere in the basement is a range of vaulted cellars and storehouses, from certain of which narrow stairs in the walling mount to the floor above. Indeed a feature of this castle is the large number of unconnected narrow stairways. The main access to the first floor is by two outside forestairs from the courtyard, one leading to the lord's quarters, the other to the retainers'. The

Lord's Hall is a handsome vaulted apartment, with a splendid double fireplace, and has been restored with modern panelling. The banqueting and/or retainers' hall alongside occupies all the lower wing at this level, an enormous chamber open to the rafters. There is no normal fireplace here, but a central hearth has been contrived, and if this was original then the smoke must have found its way out of a hole in the roofing where there is now a louvre. Particularly interesting are the kitchen premises in the west tower, at this level, consisting of the kitchen itself, with an enormous arched fireplace, area for an oven, and two slopdrains; also a handsome 'arcaded' servery, of highly modern aspect. Above this level were ample private and sleeping apartments in both towers.

The Doune of Menteith's history was inextricably linked with that of the House of Stewart. From here Murdoch, Duke of Albany, was summoned to imprisonment and then execution by the much-wronged James the First. Thereafter the castle merged with the Crown, until James the Fourth settled it on his Queen, Margaret Tudor, who died in 1525 passed it to her third husband Henry Stewart, Lord Methven, a descendant of Albany. James the Fifth granted it to another of the same line, whose grandson became the Bonnie Earl of Moray through marriage with the Regent Moray's daughter. Since then the castle has remained with the Stewart Earls of Moray. Mary Queen of Scots resided here. It was garrisoned for Prince Charles Edward by a nephew of Rob Roy, and from its walls Home, the author of *Douglas*, escaped by means of a blanket-rope.

The building was restored in 1883, and is kept in good condition by the present Earl of Moray. It is a favourite venue for visitors.

ECCLESIAMAGIRDLE HOUSE, PERTHSHIRE

This attractive and typical small fortified laird's house of the early 17th century, takes its extraordinary name from a detached portion of Dron parish in lower Strathearn, the word, locally pronounced Ecclesmagriddle or Exmagriddle, meaning the Church of St. Grill, or Grillan. Until told of its existence by a friend, the author had never so much as heard of this house or seen any mention of the lairdship in all the research he has done — a highly unusual situation. Presumably the Lairds of Ecclesiamagirdle managed to keep notably well out of all recorded history, stirring events, lawsuits, marriage contracts and the like; and the house itself is unlikely to be discovered, situated as it is within the private estate of another and more modern mansionhouse known as Glenearn House, about two miles south-west of Bridge of Earn.

Delightfully sited in a woodland setting on the south shore of a small lochan, the building conforms to the T-plan, with a main block lying east and west and the stair-wing projecting centrally southwards. The walls rise to three storeys, with the stair-wing a storey higher, to contain the usual little watch-chamber, with its own fireplace and chimney-stack, reached by a turret-stair corbelled out in the re-entrant angle, this turret having an oversailing roof. The entrance is rather unusual in being in the foot of the stair-wing but on its south front, not in the re-entrant. The doorway has a roll-moulding and is surmounted by a heraldic panel. The long north face is entirely plain save for the dormer-windows. The ground floor is vaulted and would contain the kitchen, with the Hall on the first floor, with private room alongside, and bedroom accommodation higher.

There is additional building to the west, and there has been a courtyard to the south. This is entered by an arched gateway surmounted by a panel dated 1648, with the initials S.D.C. and D.A.C., for Sir David Carmichael of Balmedie and Dame Anne, his wife.

These lands were a property of the Abbey of Lindores as early as the 12th century. Saint Grill or Grillan is said to have been one of the twelve helpers who landed with Columba at Iona. His ancient small church was in a grove of yews nearby. In its grave-yard are two Covenanting memorials, one to Thomas Small who 'died for Religion, Covenant, King and Countrie Ist September 1645'.

At the Reformation period, the lands of Lindores Abbey were

granted to Sir Patrick Leslie, a son of the 5th Earl of Rothes, who married one of the daughters of the King's illegitimate uncle, Robert Stewart, Earl of Orkney. He became Commendator of Lindores, and later Lord Lindores, and obtained Ecclesiamagirdle with the rest. He seems to have sold 'Eglismagirdill' to William Halyburton of Pitcur, and in 1629 King James confirmed a charter of the lands from Halyburton to David Carmichael of Balmedie, who presumably thereupon built the present house. One of the few references to Ecclesmagirdle appears in Macfarlane's *Geographical Collections*, of the date 1723. A rhyme, not very complimentary to the local beauties, runs thus:

> The lasses o' Exmagirdle may weel be dun,
> For frae Michaelmas to Whitsunday they never see the sun.

This, of course, refers to the situation of the place, nestling close under the northern slopes of the Ochils, denied the winter sun.

THE CASTLE, ELIE

Situated within the attractive Fife coastal resort of Elie, and overlooking the beach and harbour area, this is an early 17th century mansion of quite large proportions, with possibly an earlier nucleus, built on the L-plan and consisting of a lengthy main block lying east-and-west, of three storeys and a garret, with an oblong stair-tower projecting southwards at the west end, rising a storey higher and surmounted by a gabled caphouse and watch-chamber, this being projected on a single course of corbelling. This tower gives a greater impression of age and may well be part of an earlier building. Alongside it to the east, and probably a later addition, is a second squared tower, also gabled, providing small chambers on each of three floors. The windows of the original stair-tower are notably small, by comparison. Elsewhere on the main block they have probably been enlarged. Throughout, the gables are crowstepped and there are pedimented dormer windows at roof level. The basement is vaulted and the internal arrangements are normal for the period.

This building was apparently erected as a secondary seat for the lairds of Kincraig, an estate a mile or so to the west of Elie and Earlsferry, at one time belonging to the Bickerton family but by the time of this mansion in the possession of the Gourlays. We read that it was the house of Dr. John Gourlay, second son of Sir John Gourlay of Kincraig, who in 1657 is recorded as making a journey to Paris. The mansion is more than a mere town-house for the family; and anyway, Kincraig itself lying so near-at-hand, would not call for such a thing. It is not to be confused with Elie House, in its large grounds to the north-east of the town, a Renaissance building of somewhat later date.

Now a largely a holiday-resort, Elie was in the past a place of some note; but oddly, it was outshone in fame by its now lesser neighbour, Earlsferry, which was a royal burgh and important as the northern terminal of the ferry of the ancient Celtic Earls of Fife across Forth to North Berwick, as its name implies, a vital link in old Scotland.

INCHCOLM COMMENDATOR'S HOUSE

The Abbey of Inchcolm, on the small island of that name in the Firth of Forth, about three-quarters of a mile from the Fife coast in the Aberdour area, as an ecclesiastical building does not come within the scope of this work — even though it was, in fact, fortified latterly as defence against local pirates and English raiders both. But, as with the majority of the great lands of Holy Church, it fell to the Crown at the Reformation, and thereafter its new owners, Stewarts, added their own range of building, on the south side of the monastic quarters, including a square fortified tower, as seen in sketch. This is considerably lower than the tall abbey tower, also with its parapet and wall-walk, but with distinctive ecclesiastical-type windows.

The later tower is of four storeys, with a flat roof, rubble-walled but the parapet of ashlar. There is no attic or garret storey. The windows are chamfered, the door is on the west front and the stair is a turnpike five feet wide. It probably dates from 1609, when the commendatorship was erected into a temporal lordship for Henry Stewart, a son of the Lord Doune.

The abbey itself, of course, was very ancient, having been founded in 1123 by Alexander the First in thankful recognition of his escape from drowning in the firth when his boat sank and he managed to reach the island, and there was stranded for three days and nights in the care of a Celtic Church hermit who occupied the cell dedicated to St. Columba, or Colm, who himself is believed to have visited this island, then called Aemonia. Despite its islanded site, it became a prosperous establishment. In 1547, after the Battle of Pinkie, the English victor, Somerset, seized Inchcolm as a place from which to dominate the Forth, despatching his lieutenant, Sir John Luttrell as 'elect abbot, by God's sufferance, to utterly gain the whole use of the Forth . . . with C hakbutiers and L pioneers, to keep his house and land there, and LXX mariners to keep his waters.' The chronicler grimly adds, 'Whereby it is thought that he shall soon become a prelate of great power!'

However, the Reformation in Scotland was on its way, and with Henry the Eight's death, the English threat receded. Soon thereafter Inchcolm and its abbey were taken from the Church and given to Sir James Stewart of Beith, afterwards Lord Doune, whose son married the heiress of the Regent Moray and became himself the 'Bonnie Earl o' Moray' of the ballad, slain by Huntly at Donibristle nearby. Lord

Doune's second son, Henry, as had been indicated, was created Lord St. Colme in 1609. It seems probable that he it was who added this fortified house.

INNERPEFFRAY CASTLE, PERTHSHIRE

In a picturesque but not very strong position on sloping ground above a bend of the River Earn four miles south-east of Crieff, and near the more famous Innerpeffray Library, this is a commodious but plain fortified mansion of the early 17th century, now a roofless ruin but more or less complete to the wallhead. It is built on the L-plan, with a square stair-tower in the re-entrant angle, the main block being three storeys in height and the wing a storey higher. The walls are of coursed rubble with dressed quoins, the basement openings being mere slits, while the first-floor windows are notably large. Gunloops command the entrance, at ground- and above first-floor levels. There are no turrets. The chimney-stacks are notable, that at the wing gable, containing the kitchen flue, being large and massive, leaving room for only six crowsteps at the sides; while that serving the Hall fireplace rises from the wallhead in tall isolation on the west front. A courtyard has extended to north and west, part of the door-jamb for which still survives.

The doorway is in the foot of the stair-tower and admits to an entrance lobby, wherein is a stone bench for a porter, below the stair, and a shot-hole to command the entrance. The ingoing of this has been utilised to act as a sort of service-hatch from kitchen to stair-foot. The basement is vaulted, with the kitchen in the wing provided with a wide arched fireplace which has an oven at one end and a stone seat and aumbry at the other. There is also a stone drain — a provision also to be found in the adjoining larder. The vaulted chamber at the north end of the main block has been the laird's wine-cellar, with a private stair in the walling to the Hall above.

The main turnpike stair is wide and admits to all floors. The Hall is as usual on the first floor, and has been a fine room measuring 32 by 20 feet, and lit by the large windows on three sides. The masonry above the great fireplace in the west wall has been strengthened with a relieving arch, visible from outside. A private room adjoins the Hall, provided with garderobe and aumbry, and there was a bedroom in the wing at this level. Above, the arrangement was the same, with a withdrawing-room instead of the Hall, a comparatively late development.

Innerpeffray, like so much of Strathearn, was a Drummond lairdship. Much of the land hereabouts was Church property, belonging to the Abbey of Inchaffray, and at the Reformation the

[191]

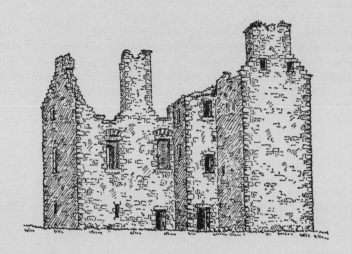

Drummonds saw to it that one of their number was secular Commendator. The lands were erected into a temporal lordship for the said James Drummond, younger and infant son of the 2nd. Lord Drummond, and in 1609 he was created Lord Madderty. He built Innerpeffray the following year. The renowned Library nearby was endowed by a bequest of David, 3rd Lord Madderty in 1691, and contains many rare and interesting books, including the pocket-Bible of the great Marquis of Montrose. Close to the Library is Innerpeffray Chapel which, since 1508, has been the burial-ground of the Drummonds.

KILBRYDE CASTLE

Although Kilbryde Castle was much altered and enlarged about a century ago, the general aspect of the original has been well maintained, and it makes an interesting and characterful mansion. It lies about 3 miles north-west of Dunblane, in South Perthshire, at a bend in the valley of the Ardoch Burn, amongst the skirts of the Highland Line, in a remote but attractive situation. The building, even before additions, was commodious, built on the favourite L-plan, of three storeys and an attic, with unusual square angle-turrets at all four corners of the main block, which runs east and west with the wing, containing the stair, projecting northwards at the west end, and rising two storeys higher. Another unusual feature is the way that the west walling has been cut back externally at the springing of the gable, to allow for a balcony or bartizan projecting slightly on corbelling, this provided with a parapet. The gables have now lost their crowsteps.

The entrance is on the north front, at the foot of the stair-wing, and gives access to a turnpike stair and also to a lateral passage-way off which four basement chambers and old kitchen open. The last occupies the south-west end of the main block and contains a wide arched fireplace in the gable. This last has the curious provision of a stone-seat at the back. The hall of drawing-room on the first floor is a fine chamber, centrally placed in the main block between a private room to the east and a diningroom to the west, this last having a garderobe off and also a serving-room in the wing, also having its garderobe. Indeed Kilbryde was usually liberally provided with such features, for on the second floor above, each of the five bedrooms is so endowed, four of them contained in the square angle-turrets. There was more accommodation in the attic floor above.

Kilbryde was originally a Graham estate, this area being part of the Graham earldom of Menteith. The castle is alleged to have been built about 1460 by a Sir James Graham, but this must refer to a still earlier building, for all to be seen today is probably at least a century later. The Earls of Menteith suffered a grievous decline in the reign of Charles the First and the property passed from the Grahams to the Campbells of Aberuchill in 1643, with the descendant of whom it still remains. This family, of the Glenorchy and Loudoun line, was given a baronetcy in 1667, and the present laird is the 8th baronet, Sir Colin Campbell of Aberuchill and Kilbryde. A predecessor, in the person of the earlier Sir Colin, Lord Aberuchill of Session, was noted for his activities against the proscribed Clan MacGregor in general and Rob Roy thereof in particular.

LENY HOUSE

Although on three sides Leny house appears to belong to the 19th century, the remaining eastern face reveals its origins as an L-planned fortalice of probably the late 16th century. Here is the typical facade of crowstepped gables and dormer-pedimented wing, which has been left unaltered, although with some small windows filled in and other enlarged. The door slapped in the east gable of the main block is modern too.

On the north face of this main block, now modernised in appearance and with all windows enlarged, at second floor level is a square red sandstone armorial panel depicting impaled arms with the initials B.F.

Internally the building has been almost entirely altered, but thick walling is evident in places and there are still two vaulted semi-subterranean chambers. The curve of the original turnpike stair in the re-entrant angle is still traceable.

At an early date there was a family of Leny of that Ilk. But in the 14th century the Leny heiress married Allan, second son of Sir Maurice, 9th Laird of Buchanan. Three generations later the Leny line again produced an heiress, and she married the 12th Chief of Buchanan. They had three sons, the eldest, Sir Alexander, being a notable soldier, killed at the Battle of Verneul in 1424. The second son then became Chief of Buchanan and the third got Leny. Eventually in 1762, when the main Buchanan line became extinct, the Leny line gained the chiefship. This was represented by the Buchanan-Hamiltons of Bardowie, Spittal and Leny, the 16th Hamilton of Bardowie's sister and heiress having married Thomas Buchanan. Their descendants retained Leny until comparatively recent times.

MONTQUHANIE CASTLE, FIFE

Set in the quiet north-east Fife parish of Kilmany, five miles north of Cupar, Montquhanie is a picturesque composition of 15th-century keep and late 16th-century and later additions, near the modern mansion. The keep is ruinous but the courtyard wing to the west is still entire, indeed recently restored, and occupied, as an attractive small dower-house.

The keep, which has been somewhat altered, is oblong and rises four storeys to a parapet and walk with open rounds at three angles. The original windows are notably small. There is no communication between the basement and the upper floors; so that the original door would be reached by a removable timber stair to the first floor. This was superseded, in the 17th century, by a handsome stone forestair from the courtyard, to the north. There is now no internal stairway, but there is a large gap in the north walling where it probably arose in a projecting tower. As neither of the two basement vaults has a fireplace, the kitchen premises must always have been in secondary courtyard buildings. The Hall, on the first floor, has a fireplace in each gable, and there are two lighted closets. The upper floors are inaccessible.

The west curtain-wall of the courtyard is incorporated in the occupied extension, built on slanting, rocky ground which dictates irregular floor-levels. It consists of a small circular flanking-tower with a conical roof, and a long two storeyed-range with crowstepped gabling. The tower, its upper part formerly used as a dovecote, is furnished with splayed gunloops of late 16th-century type, and its upper window is provided with a drip-stone. The rest of the building appears to date from about a century later.

McGibbon & Ross state that there was a heraldic lintel erected upside-down in an outbuilding, showing the Balfour arms, the initials A.B. for Andrew Balfour, and dated 1597. This could well have been the period of the flanking tower and first extensions.

'Moulhany' was exchanged by the last Earl of Fife, in the early 14th century, for Pittencrieff, with his kinsman Michael Balfour. In 1458 George Balfour signed a charter at 'Munquhane'. His grandson, Sir Michael, a favourite of James the Fourth and dying with him at Flodden, left an infant son, Andrew (above referred to) who was laird for 79 years. He had eight sons, all distinguished during the reigns of James the Fifth, Mary Queen of Scots, and James the Sixth. The third and fourth sons were respectively involved in the murders of Darnley and Cardinal Beaton. The old laird was succeeded by his great-grandson, Sir Andrew, and the estate sold about 1600. The new lairds were Lumsdens of the Innergellie line, and Major-General Robert Lumsden, a veteran of the Gustavus Adolphus wars, was captured at the Battle of Dunbar and 'very hardlie used'; appointed Governor of Dundee in 1651, and when he surrendered to the Cromwellians on honourable terms, was nevetheless slain by the English soldiery. His son sold Montquhanie to James Crawford, of the Ayrshire Auchinames family in 1676. A stone built-in to the fabric is dated 1682 with initials I.C. and M.L.

PITTAIRTHIE CASTLE

Little known because of its fairly remote and inaccessible site in the East Neuk of Fife, this is an interesting building of some size, ruinous but with the main features surviving. It is situated on high ground in open country about 7 miles due north of St. Monans and 2 south-west of Dunino. But the nearest road, B.940 Cupar to Crail, runs a mile to the south, so reaching the castle is difficult; even South Kinaldy farm is almost a mile off.

Pittairthie is a substantial L-shaped fortalice of three main storeys and an attic, with a squared stair-tower in the re-entrant angle facing south-east and a turret stair of small dimensions corbelled out above first floor level on the north front. The doorway, facing south, with a draw-bar slot, has a moulded surround and is guarded by two gunloops and two shot-holes. This multiplicity is repeated throughout the building, with almost every window provided with a shot-hole. The vaulted basement kitchen has an arched fireplace fully 12 feet wide, two aumbries in the walling and an inward sluice-basin for rain-water and an outflow through the wall.

The stair is a turnpike, leading to the hall on the first floor, as usual, which also has a basin and outflow duct, rare in such a chamber; also a finely-moulded aumbry or wall-cupboard. A yett or iron grille guards a first floor window. And over another west-facing window on this floor is built-in a former dormer pediment bearing the initials W.B. and a shield of arms which appear to be those of the Bruce family, with the date 1680.

In 1590, James the Sixth granted these lands to Andrew Murray, heir of Sir Andrew Murray of Arngask. However, he does not seem to have retained them long, for in 1598 the King grants them to Andrew Logan of Easter Granton. Again the tenure seems to have been short, for in the early 17th century we find Borthwick lairds therein. In 1644 Major William Borthwick sold the property to Andrew Bruce. And in 1654 William Bruce is returned heir to his father Andrew Bruce of Pittairthie. In the 18th century the lands were forfeited to the Crown, no doubt over the Jacobite troubles, and sold to the Cunninghames of Glencairn.

PITTENWEEM PRIORY

This is one more of those entirely secular buildings which are given ecclesiastical names because they were built immediately after the Reformation, in the second half of the 16th century, on land which had previously belonged to the Church but which was now confiscated into the gift of the Crown. Sometimes, to be sure, the existing monastic buildings were adapted or added to, but usually wholly new and fortified houses were erected by the new proprietors, for that time was well within the period when defensive houses were still considered to be necessary. So Pittenweem Priory, or Great House, is really the Commendator's residence built on the old priory site. The term commendator-prior or commendator- abbot was used frequently, so that the new secular proprietors could claim certain advantages and positions held by the former ecclesiastics, even to taking over their seats in the Scots parliament.

The present building is interesting, its plain but commodious character enhanced by sundry features, in especial the two fine oriel-type windows at first-floor level, projected on corbelling and very unusual. There is a long, three-storeyed main block, with what is scarecely a stair-tower but really only a squared projection into the

enclosed courtyard, in the foot of which is the main door. A truncated dormer-window lights the upper floor.

The priory lands of Pittenweem were in 1583 granted to William Stewart, of the Darnley family, a captain of the King's Guard, and it was later erected into a lordship for his son Sir Frederick Stewart, as Baron Pittenweem. It was however sold in 1614. The original priory dated from the 12th century, when the monks of the May Island in the mouth of the Firth of Forth, where they maintained a beacon or lighthouse, found it more convenient to live on the mainland and merely send out teams to the island. Behind the eastern entrance to the priory area, which covered nearly three acres, is the Witch Corner where Pittenweem, which was apparently much troubled by so-called witches, buried the poor creatures after grievous tortures, as late as the 18th century.

RAVENSCRAIG CASTLE, FIFE

Dramatically set on a cliff-top above the shore midway between Kirkcaldy and Dysart, this highly interesting castle is now overlooked by the high flats of the former town's expansion. It is unusual in many respects, and is said to have been the first castle in Scotland specifically designed to withstand artillery-fire, belonging to the 15th century with later additions. Partly because of the nature of the site, it does not conform to any normal plan. Two massive horseshoe-shaped towers lying to east and west are linked by a lower range, in which is the entrance, guarded by double doors, one slotted for a draw bar, and facing a bridge over a deep gully which cuts off the promontory site to landwards. The west tower seems much higher, being four storeys and an attic, while that to the east is a storey less; but because of the uneven level of the site to that side, two of its storeys are below basement level of the other. There has been considerable later work, in the 16th and 17th centuries, to seawards, terraced at varying levels, but this is wholly ruinous. The masonry throughout is of excellent squared ashlar, and the landward-facing semi-circular flanks of the two towers are of enormous thickness. A most interesting feature is the manner in which the west tower is tabled off with some slabbing at what should be parapet level; this is probably not original.

The castle was built for Mary of Gueldres, widow of James the Second, about 1460, but was never finished in its original conception, for the Queen died in 1463. It thereupon was bestowed on William St. Clair, Earl of Orkney, in partial compensation, when those islands were taken into the Scottish crown by James the Third, by the famous transaction with Norway, and the earldom changed to that of Caithness. This would account for the obvious alterations in style.

The entrance is by a narrow arched pend leading to an inner courtyard, in the lower linking building, which is in fact only one storey high, though landward its walling has been raised by a high parapet of immensely thick masonry, pierced by gunloops. On either side are vaulted cellars, and above is a platform roof, for cannon. The eastern and lower tower has a well cut in the rock floor of its vaulted basement, and the stairway is straight, in the thickness of the west wall. Its attic floor and parapet are of the 17th century.

The tall and massive western tower has been entered from a forestair at first-floor level, to the south, and a turnpike stairway rises nearby at its south-east angle. There is a comparatively small chamber on each floor because of the wall thickness, and there are many mural cupboards and garderobes. Presumably this first floor would be the Hall, somewhat inadequate as it would be for an important castle — though almost certainly it was originally planned for the Hall to be above the basements of the connecting building, where there would have been ample room. The massive chimney-stack of the Hall fireplace flue is a prominent feature of the roofline.

It is good that this interesting building, long ruinous and neglected, is now being rehabilitated.

Ravenscraig remained long the seat of the Lords Sinclair, a senior offshoot of the Caithness earldom.

TORWOOD CASTLE, STIRLINGSHIRE

This is a handsome and commodious fortalice of the seconf half of the 16th century, long ruinous but with the main features surviving. It stands on high ground about two miles north of Larbert, half a mile west of the main A9 road, with the remains of the ancient and historic Tor Wood close by. It is an L-planned building, which has had a courtyard to the north, with 17th-century outbuildings, now largely gone. The structure consists of a long main block of three storeys lying east and west, with a stair-wing projecting northwards at the west end and rising two storeys higher, to house the usual gabled watch-chamber. Within the re-entrant angle rises also a square stair-tower — not the more usual corbelled stair-turret — and this appears to have stopped short a storey lower than the wing. A tiny corbelled-out circular turret, only part remaining, carried the stair to the watch-chamber. The masonry is good throughout and well supplied with shot-holes and gunloops. There is a slight projection of the main block gable at the south-west corner, to provide flanking cover of the wall, defensively. The south face of the house is exceedingly plain, but the entrance front, to the north, compensates, with pleasing features and decorative work, including a stringcourse at first-floor level round wing and tower, and an empty panel space above the door.

The moulded doorway in the re-entrant, is guarded by gun-loops and a long slot for a draw-bar, and has a relieving arch above. The door admits to a lobby from which rises the main turnpike stair. A narrow guardroom is contrived in the wing gable, to the right. From the lobby a long vaulted passage opens along the north side of the main block, from which three cellars and the kitchen are reached, all vaulted, the kitchen being at the far east end. This is provided with the usual arched fireplace, a water inlet and a service hatch into the corridor. There is a tiny chamber off, to the north-east for purpose uncertain. The western-most basement chamber is the wine-cellar, with the usual private stair to the Hall above. There is also a small square room off, in the foot of the western projection.

Half-way up the main stair there is a vestibule contrived, with basin and drain. Higher is the Hall, a large apartment, 41 by 22 feet, having a decorative fireplace in the north wall, and a withdrawing-room off at the east end. This last has two tiny chambers hollowed out of the thick east gable, which houses the kitchen flue, and these have low ceilings, above which are windows to light the main withdrawing-room — an unusual arrangement. The upper floor, reached by the smaller stair in the stair-tower, is now ruinous, but has had dormer windows.

The courtyard, entered by a pend to the north, was extensive, and has a vaulted well-chamber at the north-east angle.

The family of Forester of Garden, taking their name from the office of keepers of the royal forest of Tor Wood, were the lairds here from the 15th century, although the present castle appears to have been built about 1566 — a carved stone to that effect being preserved in Falkirk Museum. In the 17th century the lands passed to the Forresters of Corstorphine, and it was probably this family who built the courtyard extensions. In Tor Wood, so famous strategically and as a shelter for hiding men, this castle must have seen many stirring events.

AUTHOR'S NOTE

Some small number of the ruinous buildings described herein have been, or are being, restored to make homes again — to the great satisfaction of the writer.

[207]

INDEX

[211]

[212]

[213]

INDEX TO ADDENDA